((Ring Ring))
Hello?
Grandma's House.
Big Bad Wolf Speaking.

Christmas Anthology #1

**Compiled by Sue A. Veryser-Duncan
and Slappy Cat Communications LLC**

((Ring Ring))
Hello? Grandma's House. Big Bad Wolf Speaking.

Christmas Anthology #1

Acknowledgements

Sometimes the best ideas pop into our minds at the worst times, but no matter the timing, the ideas tug at our shirttails, annoying us like a schoolyard bully until we give them our undivided attention.

With that weird analogy in mind, I give you, *A Christmas Anthology* like no other in existence. Talented writers with dreams of finally being discovered; who can't live without being able to weave their words into amazing tales, fill the following pages with stories of Christmas.

A HUGE Thank you to our sponsors **Patricia Gendernalik of Gendernalik Funeral Home, Inc., and Gene and Pam Boyd of Lakeview Powersports, and Lakiewview Motel.** Without their support the publishing and distribution of this awesome book would not have possible.

Thank you also to all of the authors who participated -- to Justin Rose, my awesome illustrator, for designing the perfect cover -- to Anne Deforest Petrous for helping me bring it all together, and for keeping me calm. Anne has been an invaluable part of the team here at Slappy Cat Communications LLC. We never would have had it ready to go to the publisher in time without her help.

And finally, thank you to my husband, who tries very hard to keep me from hurting myself when I am bouncing off of the walls, and forever listening to me jibber jabber on and on about my next great adventure! He IS a Saint!

Three Dolls

By Jay Kay -- 1995 (Janet Veryser 1936-2015)

For some reason or another, Annie could not move. "This is silly," she thought. Why even when she fell out of the apple tree (now when was that?), she still drug herself to the house and up the steps and through the kitchen door. She never cried, broken leg and all. Not till she saw Mama. Then she wailed! It's silly not being able to move. She could see out the window from where she was. It was snowing. It was always snowing. So cold.

Someone was standing next to her – face in her face. "Mama, do you know me, Mama, it's me Bethy, Mama, Mama can you hear me?"

Good Lord Child, do you think I'm deaf and blind? Of course, it's you Bethy. Santa knows where we are. He'll be coming soon. You just keep being good.

Bethy was always crying about something, especially Santa. Could he find her now that we live in the country? And to make matters worse, she'll tell Midge that we're lost and Santa won't ever come again, then Midge will cry.

I can't see out the window anymore. Guess it's dark, and so cold...

People keep coming and going – moving me around – push and shove.

Nurse Sandy says it's almost Christmas. It can't be. She's singing "Silent Night." Maybe it is almost Christmas. I've got to get my shopping done. Two little girls need dolls. I saw some pretty ones at Jacob's in the city. I'd better get going.

Boots on – coat on – I wish we women could wear pants like the men. It's a long walk to the bus, at least a mile. It's so cold.

It seems like I've done this before. Must be that Deja – Deja something.

It's cold out here – the boots don't seem to keep my feet dry.

The bus should be here soon – can't find the schedule, and I can't find my money.

Let's see now!

Oh, I'm cold – here's the bus stop. Maybe Asa will be the driver. Maybe he'll remember me and let me ride for free. Damn clothes – they don't have pockets. Who would make a coat without pockets? Makes a person wonder what the world is coming too.

Oh dear, now who's calling me? Bethy – what does she want? You can't buy presents when she's around. Always too smart; nosing about, digging in all the closets, looking under the big bed. She never found anything, but you had to give her an "A" for effort.

She never found the hiding place. That big, old black trunk in the attic holds a lot of treasures and it has a lock.

Now, if I can just get this ladder in place, I'll get to that trunk.

Nurse Sandy will help. There, now a little push and a little shove.

She's singing again. She sings them Church songs real good.

Ah, there's the trunk. Where did I put that key?

Oh – they're just like when they came from Jacob's. Pink for Bethy and yellow for Midge. They'll fight about that too.

What Sandy? "All is calm, all is bright." You know Sandy – I should have gotten three dolls – one for you in green.

I'll just go back to the store again. Now where's my boots...

I'm so cold...

Tis' The Season To Be Jolly

By Robert A. Slivatz

Scott was working afternoons at Detroit's 7th Precinct as a street patrol officer, something he thought he was best qualified after returning from SE Asia and being discharged from the Army where he'd served as a Special Forces soldier before his discharge. It was the furthest one could go in the military and it was his intent. Working the streets of Detroit seemed like the next logical step and the best place to employ his skills.

He and his partner Gomez worked Christmas Eve and then went to Gomez's in-laws to celebrate after midnight when they got off. It was an annual tradition to spend the evening with the family and there were no borders in blood between the two. Each had become the other's family shortly after meeting.

The party lasted until after 2:30 AM where they both took off. Gomez had driven as he lived close to Scott and after the midnight shift, dropped him off, and drove home to change while Scott did the same. His wife Diane gave Gomez as he arrived home with a quick kiss and had his civilian clothes all laid out ready to go. Scott's wife Lynn had done the same as they knew the routine. They were cops' wives and nothing was routine. They had exchanged their personal gifts to each other at the party as was tradition. Everyone waited for them to show up before the presents were opened, and worked it around shift changes each year.

The morning came early as Scott and Lynn got up to start the Christmas day with mass at his folks and exchanging of gifts, then over to her folks for lunch and exchanging of the gifts before Scott had to get back home, put his uniform on and go back to work. Crime doesn't take a holiday.

A quick shower to refresh himself and Scott began putting on his uniform. He checked the cylinder of the Smith and Wesson Model 10 .38 Spl to make sure it was full, as he did with his two speed loaders. He knew they were "good to go" but the checklist was always routine. He put his revolver back into the holster, handcuffs, radio holder, flash light scabbard, knife scabbard (he always carried a four inch folding blade for those emergencies and always had his Swiss Army knife in his pocket as he never went anywhere without it). He didn't wear a vest as in those days they weren't issued items and the costs were prohibitive on his salary, as he was also going to school at Wayne State University.

You needed a college education to be a Foreign Service officer which was his original goal when he was discharged. But having served time on the streets of
Detroit, the inner city was a third world country and his needs and dedication were needed most. He had grown up listening to

John F. Kennedy speak "...ask not what your country can do for you, but what you can do for your country..." and Martin Luther King Jr. speak of being "...judged not by the color of one's skin but the content of one's character..." something he had taken to heart. It was how he was raised by his parents, uncles and aunt, neighbors and family friends and mentors. Scott was a second generation airborne soldier as his father Albert had served with the infamous 82nd Airborne Division during WWII and had that never quit "all the way" instinct that was instilled into him. It's how he made it through his military training and missions. Too, he had grown up on land walked by the infamous "Roger's Rangers" who did the unthinkable with buckskins, moccasins and muskets.

   Scott always carried a Walther PPK/S inside his belt as a backup and a personal M1 Carbine with a thirty round magazine, and two fifteen round magazine in a stock magazine pouch loaded with two hollow points followed by a full metal jacket round with the last one out being a tracer so he would know when to change magazines if it ever came to that. Gomez carried the same personal M1 Carbine but with a paratrooper stock with fore grip as he liked it better in clearing houses and tight spaces. They each carried five spare thirty round magazines in their briefcase in the trunks as well as extra rounds for their handguns. Gomez carried his personal Smith and Wesson Model 19 .357 Magnum for his on duty side arm, with a Smith and Wesson Model 59 semi auto 9mm in his waistband as his backup. They had the nickname "7-2 the heavy crew" as when they showed up, hostility ceased. The number of times they heard "don't shoot me with the machine gun" was uncountable and became a catch phrase to their fellow officers throughout the department, though the M1 Carbine was standard issue if one chose to sign one out. No one knew the last time the department rifles and shotguns were cleaned and oiled, or the magazines changed, whereas Scott and Gomez were active sport shooters and knew theirs worked. The last thing Scott did was pin on the smiling Santa pin that Gomez's wife Diane got them both for Christmas for their uniforms. It felt good.

Gomez picked Scott up as he lived close and had to pass by Scott's house on the way, let alone they were partners. "Hey, long time no see" Gomez said with a smile and a laugh, "Merry Christmas again!"

"Hey, Merry Christmas again to you, old friend. It's been ages since we saw each other last. Was beginning to miss you," said Scott as they drove off laughing and making jokes all the way. The two weren't just cops, they were comedians. Plus, when they were together one never knew what would transpire.

At the precinct everyone was wishing each other Merry Christmas both to the oncoming and off going shifts. Scott and Gomez gave the boss behind the desk a cold bottle of sparkling wine with a nice red bow. Despite the streets, the officers were one big family. Yes, they had their differences as all did, and it was a mixed race force in the middle of a predominately black precinct. Prejudice was a reality on both sides, but in blue, everyone was family especially on Christmas. It felt good to be amongst those that one shared a bond that only those who have worn the badge and worked the streets could ever know. Murder, rape, robbery, burglary, and arson were the norms outside the cinder block walls of the precinct, and as is the inner city, even those walls weren't protective enough as the bad guys would be dumb enough to come in hostile to a precinct. It was a fact of life in the inner city.

The patrol sergeant just looked at Scott and Gomez's smiling Santa badges and smiled as other folks on the shift had worn ornaments similar. The sergeant was happy to see and know his officers were more than just filled uniforms but people dedicated to their job to "protect and serve" within the best of their abilities. They were not only good cops; they were good people.

They were the first precinct to get female street officers and have a female commander and it made no difference as everyone who wore the badge, earned the badge, though the women did let men handle most of the initial street talking at first, they soon had two women cars, and the transition became the norm throughout the department.

Assigned their usual car "7-2" with their nickname "the heavy crew" as their work with the carbines was well known and appreciated. Too, the other officers knew they had extra magazines and ammo in their briefcases along with extra reports, flashlights, bulbs, and batteries. Each carried a four cell aluminum flashlight, and also a "mini-mag" on their belt for backup or car work. It was much easier to use in the car then the duty size flash light. And of course their clipboards. Police work couldn't be done without their clipboards.

It was a white Christmas with about two inches of snow on the ground but the roads were clear except for the side streets. Many people had put lighted wreaths or candles in their windows inside, but no one decorated outside. They'd stripped all the abandoned homes of sinks, tubs, light fixtures, and the copper wiring in the walls that they just ripped out. You leave something outside in these neighborhoods it would likely be stolen. Most houses had bars over their windows and doors.

Their scout car area was from Mack avenue south to St. Paul, but tonight would be also covering 7-1's area as they weren't working this Christmas so it was up to the river including Belle Isle and from Mt. Elliott to Van Dyke which was the boundary between the 7th and 5th precincts and would always back each other up. Too, with the nature of the work load would be assigned runs in others' areas when they were busy. They got to know the streets, numbering processes, and all the landmarks of the main areas to automatically know the area without having to search for the crime. Time saves lives...sometimes.

They had called into service and it wasn't twenty minutes before the radio cackled "7-2 and cars in number 7, a homicide at 3615 St. Aubin, the perpetrator is still there." "Roger radio. 7-2 on the way from Field and Mack." And with that Scott turned on the lights and sirens as Gomez was driving, reached down to his right and picked up his carbine without looking as it had become a second sense, and was the extra pair of eyes for his partner as he drove as fast as possible, full attention. "Clear to the right" Scott would say at every intersection and street. Two blocks from the scene they cut off both the lights and sirens so as not to be more of a target than they already were. As they turned the corner off of Mack onto St. Aubin they could see the house, it's Christmas wreath with candle in the window, roughly eighteen inches of plywood over the bottom of the front door frame to keep the rats out, and the door slightly ajar with lights on inside.

Gomez pulled the car into a protective angle and both approached the house tactically making eye gestures to communicate they were so close in mindset. Each took a side of the door, carbines at the ready, as Gomez knocks on the open door "Good evening, Merry Christmas, did someone here call the police?"

With that they heard a response, "that's right officers, come on in, I'll give you no trouble, I just told that bitch I wasn't eating goldfish for Christmas dinner."

Gomez slowly pushed the front door all the way open with Scott's eyes everywhere taking mental snapshots and keeping his partner safe.

A tall thin man in his late fifties was casually sitting on the couch, watching TV, smoking a cigarette, a small plastic Christmas tree plugged into the corner, as there was this female body laying on the floor just in front of the TV, face down in a large pool of blood with the handle of a ball peen hammer sticking out of her head.

"Let me finish my cigarette and I'll go with you, but damn it officer go see if you'd eat that shit for Christmas dinner," said the man calmly smoking his cigarette.

Scott got on the radio as he made his way to the kitchen "radio 7-2, on scene, no other cars needed. Will need a 7-0 series and homicide."

"Will do 7-2, you say no other cars are needed?"

"Roger radio, situation has ceased hostilities however we do have a victim."

"Okay 7-2" at which time Scott entered the kitchen after visually scanning everything as one has trained and practiced. There on the stove were two large carp boiling away, head, guts and all. Scott shut the stove off. There was garbage everywhere. It was their way of life.

Gomez kept up the conversation with the man "so sir, I see you had a difference of opinion with this woman. Is she your wife?" "Yes officer, but damn, it's Christmas and I told her I wasn't eating no goldfish for dinner, but she just wouldn't listen."

Scott came back into the room and said "sir, don't worry. Where you're going I guarantee you'll never have to eat goldfish again."

"Damn straight officer and I won't have to ever listen to that damn mouth again. She just wouldn't shut up. It's Christmas, you'd think one day she could be nice, but no, she just had to go on and on to the point where I just couldn't take it anymore so I shut her up."

"Yes sir and you did a very good job of it" said Gomez.

"I'll give you no trouble officer, just let me finish my cigarette and I'll go with you. Just comes to a point where enough was enough and I had enough."

"Yes sir, I fully understand" said Gomez who then went about getting the man's name, the woman's name, and then reading him his rights, before asking any questions specific to the crime.

"I know all my rights and stuff officer and I don't care. I just told that bitch it's Christmas and I ain't eating no damn goldfish for dinner," and with that the man finished his cigarette, put it out thoroughly, slowly stood up, put his hands behind his back and said "okay officers, I'm ready to go with you."

Gomez put the cuffs on him and then asked him to please sit down on the couch and could we get him anything while we're waiting for the sergeant and homicide guys to show up as that was the procedure. The man assured him he didn't need anything else and commenced to tell the officers they'd been married about fifteen years, after being married to others, and that she just talked too much. Plus, it was Christmas where a man should be having turkey and dressing, not some goddamn goldfish. He was calm, polite and even friendly with the officers all the while his wife was dead on the floor in front of him. He either looked at the officers or watched TV as they went about making their report.

The sergeant arrived first. "Hi Sarge! Got a present for you but didn't wrap it" said Scott in his usual manner to which the sergeant just shook his head as Gomez introduced him to the perpetrator and explained the situation. It wasn't long before the guys from homicide arrived and Scott greeted them with "Merry Christmas guys!"

Gomez went over with them what he had just told the sergeant, and updated them on the investigation. As the one officer talked with the gentlemen sitting on the couch the other walked over to talk to Scott and also took a couple of pictures. The routine.

"Okay we're done here, we'll convey him downtown and you guys can wait for the coroner" was the decision of the homicide crew as usually they would have to convey the perpetrator. "Send us the reports when you type them up."

"Sir, you have yourself a Merry Christmas. Sorry you didn't have it work out the way you wanted, but these guys will take very good care of you and it was a pleasure to meet you" said Gomez as the homicide crew led him off. Scott has used the man's house phone to call the coroner and check on an arrival time which wouldn't be more than a half hour as they weren't too busy tonight. The sergeant left with the homicide crew as his job was done. A short wait for the coroner and to the station to type up their report and send it to homicide and they were back on the streets in service.

The night kept hopping, with everyone backing up everyone. The pace slowed for a bit, so they made a quick trip to Gomez's brother Jack's house. He always put out a feast and had a houseful on Christmas day. They had accepted Scott not only as Gomez's partner, but part of the family and such was the loving relationship.

Arriving in scout car Gomez naturally had to put the lights on as it was Christmas and the flashing lights were the theme of the evening. Walking into the house in uniform, PREP radios at the ready, naturally saying hello to everyone who greeted them with cheer. Being "at home" they poured themselves a shot, Gomez his scotch and Scott his brandy, went around the room saying hello to Jack's wife Julie, nephew Sean, nieces Beth and Chris, mom Dorothy and the guests that filled the house. There was celebrating, laughter and cheer all around, not just celebrating the birth of Jesus plus the holiness of Christmas, but also the celebration of family.

Jack always had a spread out fit to feed a king; turkey, ham, mashed potatoes, gravy, cranberry sauce, a variety of vegetables, pies, cakes and more. Scott and Gomez made themselves a small plate as they were just outside the precinct boundaries and should the need arise; they'd have to quickly leave. Crime doesn't take a holiday.

The gaiety felt good this Christmas night. It's always good to be around family gatherings regardless of the reason, but there is always something special about Christmas, the celebration of the birth of our Savior and a new direction for man to follow. Too, it was the holiday where everyone decorated, even the Scrooges. The city looked beautiful with its streets aglow and most folks happy and gay.

But it didn't last long. "Radio 7-2 and cars in seven, 1276 Mt Elliott a shooting in progress, multiple calls."

"Roger Radio, 7-2 on the way" and immediately they were the serious professionals off to handle the worst the city could give.

Their quick change was immediate and both moved in tandem. Gomez said a quick "goodbye folks, duty calls; tis' the season to be jolly" as Scott had the door open and was making his departure.

Jack was a banker and older than Gomez. A very wonderful straight gentleman who always saw the good in everything and the quick change in nature took him by surprise. He'd never seen a transformation so complete without delay. It so moved him, he talked about it every deer season for years, and most family gatherings. He was never surprised at anything that ever came out of those two. He had learned the unexpected should be expected. This one remained with him forever, and was also a story at every Christmas as everyone noticed the change in appearance and stature and it had imprinted into their psyche.

Gomez and Scott were two in body but one in spirit. Each could read the others mind. There wasn't always the need for small talk. Gomez driving and Scott being his eyes to the right, the standard method of operation, getting there as fast as one possible, and as safe as possible, as nobody wanted to get hurt. Gomez and Scott were seasoned and very good at what they did.

The change in neighborhood decorations was noticeable as they crossed back into the precinct, along with the multitude of abandoned homes.

The route was direct and as they arrived so did scout 7-3 with the Godfather and the Sarge working together. Godfather carried a department shotgun whereas Sarge (nicknamed for his rank as serving a tour in Vietnam with the 3rd Brigade of the 82nd Airborne Division before becoming a cop) carried his personal custom High Standard Model 10 with pistol grip and built in high lumen light and shoulder guard.

As they neared, again, they shut off their lights and sirens so as to not give their direct arrival away, and come with some sense of surprise, the only tactical advantage they had outside of their training and experience.

Many of the neighbors were peeking out and pointed to the house in question, their lights off, some opening their door to let the police know they heard the shooting "multiple shots," they quietly informed the cops.

Godfather went and immediately covered the rear, as the others made themselves covered each side of the door.

"POLICE! OPEN UP" said Gomez as he wrapped the door with his flashlight, and the door moved. Immediately the officers entered in synch with tactical movements. The lights were on, as was the TV as one man was sitting in a chair across the room with a revolver in one hand and a bottle in the other, while across from him sat another man upright in the chair, his boots off in front of him, and obviously shot many times.

"Put the gun down first sir, we need to talk" to which he looked up and saw the two carbines and the twelve gauge pointed at his head, the light blinding him in the process.

He didn't move immediately as it was obvious he was greatly intoxicated, but he still had a revolver in one hand, and the officers wanted to make it home safely, and also take this man safely.

Gomez's talking and the Sarge's light from his High

Standard Model 10 in his eyes, confused him, slowed his already intoxicated movements, which Scott was in position, and quickly grabbed his arm with the revolver, knocking it to the floor and getting the man into an arm lock. Gomez and the Sarge immediately got his other arm and placed the cuffs on him. He was secure. Scott immediately secured the .38 Spl revolver from the floor and checked the cylinder noting all six rounds had been fired.

"Radio 7-3."

"7-3 go ahead."

"Yes we're here on the Mt Elliott with 7-2. No other cars needed. We have a victim and the perpetrator is in custody. We're going to need a 7-0 unit and homicide"

"Roger 7-3, thanks, will have them on the way."

Gomez and the Sarge read the man his rights and then went on to question the perpetrator while Scott was busy searching the rest of the house. Finding them the only two in the house and all else secure, he shined his light out the back window alerting the Godfather that all was clear.

When the Godfather came in he said "damn, what happened to this dude?"

The Sarge turned to his partner and explained to his partner "it seemed his brother's feet stunk."

"What you say?"

The perpetrator seems to have been drinking all day and his brother had to work a twelve-hour overtime shift, got home, sat down in the chair and took his boots off. They argued about his feet stinking and his one brother not working while he was out slaving all day, so his brother emptied his .38 Spl into him."

"Man what's wrong with you?" said the Godfather. "Fool, don't you know this is Christmas and it tis' the season to be jolly?" "Now why you go and shoot up your brother like that?"

"I told you cops, his feet stunk. I don't care if he worked or not but I just couldn't put up with that smell!" said the perpetrator.

"But he was your brother!" said the Godfather.

"Not anymore!" said the perpetrator.

"You good here?" asked the Sarge to 7-2.

"Yep, we got it here except for the paperwork. Appreciate the backup," said Gomez.

"We're brothers man, and we always backup our own," said the Godfather.

"Well, look on the bright side, the guy even drunk is a pretty good shot," said Scott. "He gave six pieces of lead for his Christmas present."

"Ho, Ho, Ho, tis' the season to be jolly; Merry Christmas guys!" 7-3 said as they left.

Traditionally Speaking

by Angela Mercer-Penny

Every family has Christmas customs, rituals that they carry out, year after year, over the holidays. For some, it can be things that we did as kids that we now do with our own. My kids get to open one present on Christmas Eve, exactly the same as I did every year as a child.

But my favorite Christmas tradition was one that I didn't even know we were creating, and it's now become my most treasured part of the season.

Many years ago we were living away. It was the first time we had ever been away from home, and although we weren't ready, Christmas was still approaching. On December 15 we had moved into a new place, and didn't even have curtains in all the windows, let alone a Christmas tree. There were more bills than money, and I wasn't sure how we were ever going to make Christmas happen for the kids. It was a pretty bleak month.

Two of my sisters and my nephew came to stay with us for Christmas, and it was the greatest blessing. We had family, finally. Maybe it wouldn't be so lonely.

But more than just having them there, they took it upon

themselves to stock the fridge and freezer for us. We were more than appreciative. One of my sisters took me shopping, and while we pushed around 2 shopping carts filled with gifts, I can remember thinking, "How can I ever repay her for this?" She assured me that she wanted to do this, that she had gotten a bonus at work and she was happy to share.

You know, every Christmas since that year I think about what she did for us and our kids, and it wasn't many years later that I realized that I could never repay her for what she did, but I could pay it forward. With our money and our friend's help we adopted a family of 7 kids and made the best Christmas ever for them. Through tears, I sent her an email describing what she had done for us that year and told her she was the reason that these kids would have an amazing Christmas and full bellies.

Back to that Christmas so many years ago....The kids really wanted to do some shopping of their own, but I just didn't see how we could afford it. I tried to convince them to make something from the craft supplies we had at home, but they didn't want to. They wanted money to shop and pick out appropriate gifts for their family. It was a huge source of stress for me. I understood, but I just didn't know what I could do.

We had about $20 that we could give them to shop, but they wanted to buy 6 presents each, so everyone who would be with us on Christmas morning had something to open. We went to the only place you can buy 12 presents for $20, the dollar store. They marched in with a list and their money, did their shopping and even managed to buy wrapping paper and gift tags and tape to wrap their carefully chosen gifts.

I had no idea that 2 kids and $20 could bring me so much joy, but the experience was magical.

Every gift that they picked out had a special meaning for the recipient. They put a lot of care and thought into everything they bought.

I think, by far, our favorite gift that year was the nutcracker that my daughter bought for her father. We stared at it quizzically when he unwrapped it. A shiny metal nutcracker...until she said it was a tool for work. He was working as an electrical apprentice at the time, and in her 4 year old mind, this shiny new tool was perfect for her father.

If you check his tool pouch today, sitting amongst the pliers and measuring tape, hammer and pencils, is a little silver nutcracker. Still his favorite tool.

We had so much fun opening those gifts that we decided to do it again the next year, and the year after, and I couldn't imagine a Christmas morning now without those dollar store presents. It has become a tradition in our family, a little magic born out of meager times.

So this year, after the tree is up, and the mood is set, I will take two, unwilling and grumbling teenagers to the dollar store, with their little brother in tow, and they will pretend to hate the experience, like teenagers do. But I know that later on, when they have kids of their own, they will love their own dollar store gifts as much as we do.

It is easy to say that Christmas isn't about the gifts, it's not about the money you spend, or the things you buy. It's easy to say that while you can afford to do it. But in the lives of two broke young parents, it felt like our hardships meant that we were somehow failing our kids back then. We had no idea that out of our struggle, we were given the most humbling of gifts. The gift to experience the tradition of Christmas magic.

The Kitchen Sink

by Tammy Williams

On the side of the box were the words" The Kitchen Sink". In every sense this was an ordinary box for a Christmas present, it was brown, no colored ribbon, no Santa clause wrapping paper, just plain like in the old days. The only thing normal about this Christmas present is that it was a box.

No one in my family would every guess that the plain ordinary box would once again have us believe in the spirit of Christmas. My mom always gave me Christmas in July every year because, she lived in Montana. The winters were brutal and for her to get out and mail the present was not possible for an elderly lady. Mom with her gray hair and laugh wrinkles, giggled the first time she gave me the box with her writing on the side. After receiving" The Kitchen Sink", I put the Christmas gift in the back room for its opening in December. The kids of course were curious and wanted to know what was in the box and why did she write the words "The Kitchen Sink" on the side? I could not answer those question so, I just shrugged and said" we will have to wait for Christmas Eve when we open presents".

The first holiday to come was Halloween and The kids and I felt frustrated by the fact the department store was putting Christmas junk out before Halloween. I mumbled under my breath," how can they be so insensitive towards the other

Holiday? As if Halloween had feelings. I laughed out loud with that thought and my son said "I agree mom", as if he knew my thought. As a single parent, my kids and I love the holidays and love to decorate but money was always short. Halloween decorations consisted of a jelly looking witch and black cat laying on the window of my front door.

Carving pumpkins for Halloween is always a great time to create a mess so, I went to the back room and I moved the box with the words "The Kitchen Sink" to the side to get some bags for the Halloween pumpkin seeds. I stopped and ponder what on earth could my mother be up to? What does she mean by "The Kitchen Sink"? Hope she didn't give me a sink!

Craving pumpkins with the kids is so much fun and as we get older I think we lose that wonder we had as a child in the mist of our older age. Stuffing our seeds into the bags, the conversation that pursued was not of Halloween but what is in "The Kitchen Sink"? My youngest son suggested an x box, TV, afghans, a big rock. I told the kids it was a kitchen sink, my daughter thought it might by a TV since she shook the box and informed me that whatever it was, it was heavy, like a TV and that the words "The Kitchen Sink" was to throw us off. We finished our pumpkins and placed them on the front steps, still wondering what "The Kitchen Sink" consisted of?

Halloween came and went and we all gained 5lbs from the

candy. Our next holiday was Thanksgiving and the opportunity to share our bounty with others so, I invited the old man next door for dinner. Our family loves Thanksgiving not only for the reason to eat but, the Christmas tree comes out on black Friday and we decorate. The ordinary present "The Kitchen Sink" as we now called it was the main topic at dinner. The conversation drifted into what we all wanted for Christmas my son wants an Xbox ™, my daughter is convinced that "The Kitchen Sink" a TV just because, if it's a new TV she gets the one in the living room. I know my mother and she is up to something. Our guest asked us what "The Kitchen Sink "was and my children brought the ordinary Christmas present out and he laughed.

As our guest help himself to another piece of pumpkin pie, we asked our guest if he knew what might be in the now mysterious box known as "The Kitchen Sink"? He laughed again and said "yes" but, it's a gift and he isn't going to spoil the spirit of this Christmas by telling us what it was.

The gift, seemed to preoccupy everyone's mind on black Friday. We all took turns shaking it trying to be as gentle as possible just in case it was a TV. Hanging the last of the garland and placing the ordinary Christmas gift in the back part of the tree we just stared at it no words came to mind, curiosity took over and we were mesmerized by the fantasy of the possibilities of this gift. As my mind wondered into a new TV scenario the phone rang. It was my mom.

"Hello Mom" I said, in my mind I wondered if she knew I was thinking of the gift. She asked straight away "Did you open the box yet?" I answered "No, Mom we are waiting for Christmas eve."

Mom went on to tell me about the winter storm that just concluded and how many inches of snow they just got in Montana. She went on about my siblings and, I asked if they received a box like mine, she said "No". I am her favorite, made me smile to think I was the only one in the family to get that special box but then again was I? Was I being set up by my mom on a horrible re gift? Yikes! Maybe I am not her favorite and its a cruel joke maybe it's a box within a box within a box within another box and in the tiniest small box was a kitchen scrubber?

After hanging up the phone with my mom, I became obsessed with the box, looking at it from different angles, shaking it just a little just in case it was a TV, but that made no sense mom would never spend that much money on a gift. What is in the box?

As my obsession and curiosity grew, I brought in an expert my best friend Anna. I informed her of the mysterious Christmas present called "The Kitchen Sink". She looked at it and all she could say in her southern draw was "what in the world?" Anna has never heard of such a box but my older neighbor did? Nothing made sense when it came to the box and I mean nothing! It was ordinary, no bow, no wrapping paper just a plain box with the words "The Kitchen Sink". The box has me stumped! I will just have to wait for Christmas eve, but in the meantime Christmas baking must commence.

December is such a great time of year, the parties, the food, the presents and now the gift "The Kitchen Sink" that has everyone in my circle of friends talking about. We all have an opinion of what's in the box. Ed (my neighbor) says it's a gift for the kids, his wife says it's an heirloom of sorts, personally I think my mom has officially lost it and I spoke up and told everyone she just gone stark raving mad! A thunderous laugh came and we all enjoyed the rest of our evening with games. The night ended and for some reason I said goodnight to "The Kitchen Sink" as if it was an old friend staying the night.

Christmas eve was coming one more week and the kids and I could do nothing but talk about "The Kitchen Sink". At this point all I could think about was please don't let it be a kitchen scrubber in a small box.

Christmas Eve day was finally here; we always celebrate with a big Christmas eve party. All the baking was done, all the gifts were wrapped, and in the back corner sat "The Kitchen Sink". Finally, we get to see what was in that mysterious box but, we all had to wait until our guest have left. A fun evening was upon us and we laughed and played games and finally our guest left. The kids at this point were chomping at the bit to see what was in the box.

First, I passed out all the gifts to the children, even though we were all wanting to see what was in "The Kitchen Sink". I was saving it for the last gift a grand finally to the night. My daughter opened her presents to find a necklace in graved with her name and a lovely sweater next, my son opened his gifts and he got a hand held game, and a bike. My turn, I opened the present from my children and I got a lovely necklace. I said "thank you" then told them that "I Loved the necklace and them". As much as my children wanted an x box and a TV they knew I was a single parent and times were hard. We all hugged and with a big scream we all said "Let's open The Kitchen Sink!"

At last the mysterious box with no ribbon, and no fancy wrapping paper was scooted out from the back of the Christmas tree. For a moment I didn't want to open it. Why? I loved this box all these months. Contemplating what was in it. Then I knew before I even opened it what was in the box, it was Christmas Spirit. No matter what was in the box it gave our family the Christmas Spirit.
I opened the box and could not believe my eyes, there in front of me was a mound of junk. Items that were sitting around my

mom's house that I recognized. With bewilderment I pulled out
a jacket that belong to my late father, a platter, some beads, a
vase with fake flowers, Christmas platters, an apron, Windex,
and last but not least a half a roll of toilet paper.

We laughed and laughed and laughed through the rest of the
night. What a wonderful gift my mom gave us both in spirit and
in fun. I called mom and asked her "Why did you write "The
Kitchen Sink" on the side of the box? Her answer was simple an
old saying everything but the kitchen sink was in that box. We
laughed over the phone and said "I Love You's and Merry
Christmas "

Every year, we got "The Kitchen Sink" until I believe my mom
ran out of junk to give us. I guess it was her way of throwing
things out she just could not part with and thought I could
provide a new home.
My children and I talk about that mysterious box known as

"The Kitchen Sink" and laugh and are grateful for that gift and
how it brought back the Christmas spirit in our house. It' s not
the money, or how fancy a gift, or how many gifts you get, it's
the love of family that will remain in your heart also known as
the Christmas Spirit.

Grandma Grama Kashuesta and the Magic Cookie

by Laura Veryser

It fell down, down, down to the ground below-- tumbling and spinning –- whirling and twirling. The wind blew it around until it met the other flakes, which were busy blanketing the Earth with their cold whiteness. It was at this time of year, when the winter would set in around us, that my nieces would climb up into my lap and request a story to be told to them. The cold sniffle-inducing air would not let them roam the outdoors the way summer would and so it became my task to entertain their minds.

The stories never came from real story books and never could -- not with me reading them.

We are old enough to read to ourselves, Aunt Warwee," *Mandy would explain. "We want to hear tales never told* *before," and with that she would select a cook book or the* *dictionary from which my imagination should be the legend.*

On this particular day, after I was accosted by the youthful *gnomes and put to rest in an over-stuffed corner chair, a large* *red and white checked cookbook was selected from the shelves* *and plopped into my lap. It promised an interesting read,* *what with its pages falling out and crumbling to the touch. The little hands that had selected it, left their marks on the dusty cover, which was quickly relieved of its aged powder as one of my jailers blew the dust off the cover towards my body. They giggled as I frantically coughed and waved my arms in the air to keep the majority of dust from entering my nose. The floating particles soon settled elsewhere as my arms were restrained by the two small bodies that leaned upon them. I was fluffed and rearranged for their maximum comfort and they paid little or no attention to which way my arms, torso and legs were really meant to bend.*

The musty old book was opened to the dessert section, Cassy's favorite chapter, and the recipe of the choice was selected.

"There," Cassy pointed at a picture. "Tell this one," she licked her lips at the sight.

A large plate of cookies was the main subject of the picture (at least, to the girls it was) with a glass of milk and some small sandwiches which decorated the foreground. In lieu of the fact that the pictures had no color to t hem, the girls were quite intent on creating their own palette of cookie colors.

Knowing full well what they wished to hear, I began to read, "2 cups of flour, 1 cup of water, ½ cup of sugar..."
"NO!" they both shouted in unison.

"You're so weird Aunt Warwee," Mandy scolded me while wagging her finger in my face. "Read it correctly."

"You do know that my name is not Warwee, don't you?" I asked her scrunched up face. "It's Laura. I don't call you Manwee."

"That's not my name," the scowl left her face, and she leaned back smiling.

"Yes, I know that's not your name, but my name is not Warwee," I replied again.

"Yes it is," she said content. Her sister laughed.

Once, a long time ago...I began.

"How long ago? 1000 years ago?" Mandy asked.

"2000 years ago?" Cassy entered the discussion.

"No, not that long ago. More like 20 years ago."

"When you were free?" Cassy asked.

"When I was what?"

"Free!" She held up three fingers.

"Oh three!" I exclaimed, understanding the visual aid.

"If you were only three, how could you remember this story? You had to be older!" Mandy demanded.

"Okay—look, it is not a true story," I said adjusting my sleeping legs.

"It's not," she gasped clutching my face in her hands.

"No, it's not," I mumbled.

"I don't want to hear it then if it is not real." Mandy huffed.

"All right, we'll make it a true story that didn't happen to me."

"Let's start this different, okay? And no interrupting me unless it is important.

Now, as I said before, winter was settling in..."

"You didn't say that before," Mandy protested.

"Shhhhhh – just listen."

Winter was settling in, around and on the small northern town of Littleton. The snow fell down from the graying heavens above to the whitening ground below, and those flakes fell fast – tumbling and spinning—whirling and twirling. As night into morning progressed, the flakes grew from tiny wisps into large and thick droppings, pelting the Earth, and with the weather so cold and the wind so blustery, everything began to freeze. It was decided two hours before school was to begin, that it should remain closed for the day.

"It just wouldn't be fair for the children to brave this atrocious weather," the school master decided, starring out the window, so he kicked off his slippers and hopped back into his warm, cozy, comfortable bed. The children did the same, jumping back in their own warm beds after a brief jump for joy.

Pip sat perched at his usual spot, the front window, to watch the sleepy, now snowed, little town come to life. He smoothed out his whiskers after his morning milk, which Grandma had so kindly warmed. The kettle whistled out, beckoning Grandma back to the kitchen for her cup of tea. She patted Pip's fluffy black back as she rose from her seat by the fire. Pip meowed his appreciation, and returned to his entertainment of gazing out the frosty window pain.

Hours later, shaking off their extra hours of sleep, the children clumsily bounded from their doorways, braving the "atrocious weather." They were all wrapped tight in their matching winter best, all, that is, except for Steven...

"Hey, that's our brother's name," Cassy blurted out, breaking the silence that had only lasted less than two minutes.

"Yes, I know that."

"That's our Dad's name too," Mandy added

"Yes—I know that too, but as I would like to finish this story sometime this year, I will continue..."

Steven was wearing the usual mismatched blue snow pants and orange coat that he had worn for the past two years, and to top off his monstrosity of fashion, his mother wrapped his face tight with a red scarf and plopped a brand new, bright blue stocking cap upon his head. All in all, the boy was a poor sight to the eyes, well, all eyes except for little Mikel Dee, his next door neighbor and best friend. See, Mikel was color blind – whatever we called orange, he saw some other color, yet still called it orange—so he didn't know what a terrible mass of colors Steven appeared to be every winter day. Unfortunately, all the other kids in town knew Steven's color problem, and every day they'd let him know, too.

Pip loved to watch Steven and Mikel play, and it was easy to do from his spot in the window, because Steven and Mikel lived across the street from Grandma.

"Oh, those were the days," Pip purred to himself, and rolled over on his back to scratch that itch he could never seem to reach. He began to daydream of the days when he was a young kitten – so full of energy—running through the fields – stalking the mice – and this particular day, he dreamed of those wintery days when he and his best friend, Kinwell, would play hide-n-seek in the snow banks. "Yes, those were the days," he declared again, not knowing whether it was the youth or the friendship that made him long for the past. Worn out from his memories, he deserted his place at the window for a more sleep-inviting place next to the fireplace.

"The cat can talk?" Mandy asked.

"No," I decided, "but he can think."

"How do you know what the cat was thinking if he can't talk?"

Anyway –Steven emerged from his house all smiles at the seemingly perfect day ahead of him – no school and lots of snow –what could go wrong? He muddled through the deep banks of snow to Mikel's front door in order to gather his friend for a day of frozen wonderment. The boys decided to build a snow fort.

"Two levels," Mikel suggested, dumping another wheel barrow of snow onto the pile.

"How about we make an igloo with separate rooms off to the sides?" Steven contributed a shovel full of snow to the heap.

"What if you just stick to one level and one room today?" Steven's Mom asked while delivering hot chocolate to the construction workers in her front yard.

The boys agreed and began to mold their one room, one level, igloo, and after a few breaks to eat lunch and toss snowballs at each other, they finally finished. It wasn't the greatest looking snow hut on Earth, but it served its purpose –fun. Setting up the essentials inside – a radio, blanket, deck of cards, thermos of hot cocoa with marshmallows, and two cement blocks for chairs – the boys moved in.

After a few rousing games of Go Fish, Steven and Mikel relaxed on the cold icy floor of their fort. They talked about school, teachers, dreams and wishes.

"I wish I could see better," Mikel whispered dreamily. See, not only was Mikel colorblind, he also wore glasses as thick as the ice was that day.

"He couldn't wear glasses that thick, Aunt Warwee," Mandy shook her head; "They'd be too heavy."

"It's called exaggerating."
"When are we going to talk about the plate of cookies?" Cassy sighed.

"Soon, if you'd let me finish."

So, Mikel told Steven of his dream to see better, and Steven hoped his friends dream would come true. Thinking very hard, Steven stared at the ceiling and sighed "I wish people liked me."

"I like you," Mikel proclaimed.

"I know you like me, but I want other people to like me."

"My mom likes you and so does my dad," Mikel offered.

"No, you see, I want other kids in town not to pick on me. I want them to like me. I want to be popular."

"Good luck! They're only nice to me because my Dad's the only police officer in a town that doesn't have many criminals. He's got lots of time on his hands," Mikel laughed, but inside he felt bad for his friend. Mikel could testify that the other kids in the town were never nice to Steven, so could Pip.

The sun was setting on the little town, and the two little boys, in the house of ice, laid quietly, watching out a hole in their roof for the first star of evening to arrive, when Steven's mom called him in the house.

"Steven, Steven? Could you come in here a second?" she beckoned him from the front porch.

Assuring Mikel he'd be right back, he ran to his mother's side, hoping she'd be calling him for something good – like food. She had a plate in her hand all right, but it wasn't for the boys – No – it was for the lady across the street!

"Steven, can you and Mikel take this across the street to Mrs. Kashuesta? I'm afraid with this weather she might not have all the provisions she needs," she handed him the plate, but Steven would not take it.

"I ain't going there. She's a pretty scary lady," Steven said wide eyed.

"Oh nonsense!" she exclaimed, passing him the plate again.

"Now GO!" She turned her son around and gave him a little shove.

Steven whined at her, but did as he was told, stopping first to get Mikel. He climbed inside the igloo to give Mikel the bad news and to talk him into coming along to meet his doom.

"I ain't goin' with you," Mikel said scowling.

"Awe – Come on!" Steven pleaded in a very whiney voice, "I don't want to die alone."

"I don't want to die at all."

Steven set the plate down so he could perform more intense begging of his friend. "Please, Mikel, we have a better chance of escaping if we go together."

"No way, Man." Mikel refused, shaking his head. "My oldest brother, Sam, told that when he was my age, his best friend went over there and disappeared forever. They say that she locks kids up in a basement and feeds them lots and lots of food until they get really big – like five pounds. Then she sicks her black cat on them, and he steals their breath so they will die. After they're dead, she stuffs them in a giant freezer in the basement and uses them for food."

"You don't know that," Steven dismissed his tale.

"You ever wonder why you never see her outside or anywhere

else. She never goes to the grocery store – she has all the food she needs in her basement, and when she runs out, she gets another kid to come over."

"That's disgusting!"

"Yeah, Aunt Warwee, that's very gross. How could you make up a story so disgustin'?" Mandy asked

"What do you mean? This story is not made up. You requested a real one." I said in my serious voice. The girls squirmed in my lap.

"Yeah, it's disgusting, but it's true – I swear," Mikel crossed his heart.

"I don't believe you."

"Why do you think that cat is always watching us? It's getting old. It needs a new life, and we're it."

Steven brushed off Mikel's spooky talk and picked up the plate, "I'm just going to go over, ring the bell, set the plate down and leave."

Mikel laughed, "It'll never work. Listen, I'll go with you, if we get captured, I get the softer bed and warmer blankets."

The two young lads, frightfully crossed the street, the plate of food was held tight in Steven's quivering hands. Mikel brought up the rear of the twosome. He was "watching Steven's back" or at least that's what he said. In all actuality, he was hiding behind him – ready to turn and run home at a moment's notice. They reached her front sidewalk and paused, gazing up at the old house.

"Look! There's a light on in the attic. Maybe that's where she keeps the kids," Mikel wondered out loud.
His comment made Steven's uneasiness heighten, as the boys' feet were about to touch the first step to their doom. Their teeth began to chatter as Steven reached for the doorbell. He pressed it, and the boys waited – there was no answer. So he pressed it again – still no answer.

"Maybe she doesn't need any more food," Mikel whispered, clutching tight to his friend's coat and peaking around his head.

"No, look. The little sign says, 'please use back door' Come on, let's get this over with." Steven huffed. "That would make it easier for her to lock us away. I bet her basement stairs are right by the back door." Mikel theorized, still hiding behind Steven.

They were rounding the back of the house, Steven exclaiming

how paranoid Mikel was, when they saw her.

She startled the boys, who did not expect her to be in the backyard. Well, the plate of food flew straight into the air as they howled out in fright.

"Were the cookies on that plate?" Cassy asked.

"What cookies?"

"The ones in the picture."

"No, we haven't gotten to that part yet."

"Good, I was afraid they had ruined the cookies!"

"As I was saying…"

The boys were scared stiff, all the rumors of her had caught up in their imagination.

"Hello," she cooed in her nicest old lady voice.

Pip, who was out with her, ran to the place where the boys were frozen and rubbed up against their legs. Mikel almost wet his snow pants, and Steven's knew knocked together in fright.

"I didn't mean to startle you," she explained, slowly walking closer to them. "I was just out here looking at the evening star – the one you wish upon." Pip kept up the leg rubs and Grandma continued, "I wasn't expecting any company, and especially not two young boys to be throwing a plate of food around."

Steven and Mikel were shocked – she looked nothing like what they had imagined. They thought she'd be tall and lanky with ghostly white skin and slimy green hair. She laughed at the image they had in their head—she Grandma had a special skill for reading people's thoughts.

"Oh, she was psycho!" Mandy announced.

"No, she was sort of psychic."

"Oh!"

She scratched her head on which her fluffy white hair sat. She knew very well that the boys were on their way over that is why she put the kettle on and had begun baking up a treat.

"The cookie?"

She moved closer to the boys who were still unable to move. "You may already know this, but I'm Mrs. Kashuesty –you can call me Grandma Grama. You must be the kids from across the street, Steven and Mikel?"

"Y-y-y-yes!" Steven stuttered. "I-I-I'm Steven and he's Mikel."

"Nice to finally meet you boys. My cat loves to watch you play. His name is Pip." She said, pointing to the cat. Pip sat his chubby body up on his hind legs, and waved his paws in the air.

"Anyway, I was looking for the first star of the evening. I had a little wish to make but it seems that the sky won't clear enough for me to find it." The kitchen kettle announced it was boiling and Grama ran to pull it off the stove. "I made a big batch of cookies," she called out to the boys," she called out to the boys from her back porch. "It may be hard to believe, but I can't eat them all," she exclaimed rubbing her round belly. "Would you both like to help me eat them?" She went in the house not waiting for an answer.

"I've heard this story, Steven. Do the names Hansel and Gretel ring a bell?" Mikel asked.

"I don't know," Steven said, surfacing from his frightened feelings. "She seems okay to me. Anyway – I'm hungry and dinners not for another two hours at my house. Come on, let's go inside," Steven pressured Mikel.

Hemming and hawing, Mikel finally agreed. They climbed the

back porch steps and entered Grama's back door. "Please forgive the mess," she told the boys while pouring three cups of hot cocoa made from real candy bars. She told the boys to have a seat at the thick, round, wooden table in the center of the kitchen, and to help themselves to the cookies on the plate.

"Yea, the cookies," Cassy interrupted.

Steven decided to make conversation, so he asked, "What were you wishing for, Grandma Grama?"

She sat down at the table across from them her green eyes sparkled, "Well now, if I told you, my wish, it would never come true."

"We'll tell you ours, if you tell us yours," Mikel chimed in.

"So you two have wishes as well, hum," she pondered placing a thinking hand under her chin. "See you can't tell me your secret wishes, and I can't tell you mine because we want them all to come true." She reasoned out loud. "Ah-ha! I've got it," she jumped up out of her seat and went over to the cupboards. "Let's see – let's see. Hum, where did I put that special sugar. Ah! Here it is," she pulled it out of the tall cupboard and blew off the dust. Pip curled up in Steven's lap, and meowed until the boy began to pet him. "My mother gave this to me and her mother gave it to her and so on."

"Is it still good?" Mikel asked screwing up his face in a look of disgust.

"Yes it is, Mikel. Special things like this never go bad." She smiled brightly.

"What does the special sugar do?" Steven asked with his mouth full of cookies.

"The special sugar makes secret wished come true," Grama explained pulling another cookie sheet out of the oven.

"Do you just eat the sugar and your dreams come true?" Mikel wondered turning the bottle around in his hands. It was just an ordinary bottle that said "Special Sugar" on it and nothing else. The sugar inside was finely ground and looked like the new snow that was currently beginning to all from above.

She called the boys over to the stove where she had just placed the hot cookie sheet. Upon it was a large cookie shaped like a person – with two little arms and legs and a little head. "Now, the Special Sugar only works when sprinkled onto a large, freshly baked cookie shaped like a person," she explained. The boys were intently listening. "You take a pinch of sugar and you place it somewhere on the person, all depending on what you are wishing for. For example: if you want to obtain more friends, you sprinkle some on the hands, if you want to change something on your body, say your eye color, you sprinkle it where the eyes would be and so on. But, in order for it to come true, you have to make your wish while you are sprinkling it and then when it cools you must eat the piece you decorated."

Well, the boys were eager to do this, and so Mikel took some Special Sugar and sprinkled it on the eyes—wishing that he didn't have to wear these big glasses any more. Then, Steven took some and sprinkled it on the hands – wishing he could make more friends who wouldn't pick on him. Finally, Grama took a pinch and sprinkled it on the heart – wishing she could have more visitors she could give her love to. Pip wanted in on the wishing action and Grama sensed it. She flipped the cookie over and sprinkled some Special Sugar over the heart, on the back – Pip wishing he could go back in time to see his old pal Kinwell again. The three, actually four, sat at the kitchen table anxiously awaiting the cookie to cool, and when it did, Grama served them each the piece they had wished upon. The boys gulped theirs down.

"It won't happen right away, "Grama warned them. "It may take hours, a night, a couple days – one never knows."
The boys were having so much fun with her they didn't even notice how long they had stayed there. They polished off the batch of cookies she had made, sticking a few in their pockets for later. When they left, Grandma Grama Kashuesta made

them promise they would come back every day until their wishes came true, and they agreed to the deal. After all, she did give them a bite of the magic cookie. That night they slept sounder and happier than ever before as they dreamed of those things they thought would never come true.

When Mikel awoke the next morning, he still needed his glasses. He walked out to the kitchen where his mom was cooking the family breakfast. He told her all about what happened last night and how excited he was.

"Mikel, you came home so late last night, I forgot to give you these," she said handing him a box, "your father stopped and picked them up yesterday."

Mikel tore open the box. His wish had come true – he didn't have to wear his glasses anymore – he had contacts. They had ordered them in his prescription two weeks earlier but he had forgotten,

School was open again, and Mikel couldn't wait to show everyone his new un-glasses. He raced over to Steven's house to show him the magic cookie worked. As they stood at their bus stop, Mikel noticed Grama peeking out the window at them. He franticly pointed at his eyes, and she smiled, knowing exactly what he meant by it.

She hoped it would be Steven's turn next, but when the boys arrived at the school, things were just like they were before. Mikel reminded Steven how his wish had come true, which gave him a little ray of hope. They entered their third grade classroom, and noticed all the kids had objects on their desks.

"Show-n-tell," Steven had forgot. So had Mikel, but he could improvise with his new contacts.

Steven thought and thought of what he would say, and then he stuck his hand in his coat pocket. In there, hidden under his mittens, was a piece of magic cookie. He knew what to do, and when it came his turn, he stood up in front of all those people who called him names, and he shared his secret. He told them all about how scared they were to go over to Mrs. Kashesta's house, and how she had frightened them, He told them about Pip, and the hot cocoa made with real candy bars. Then, he told them about the magic cookie with the Special Sugar, and most important, he told them about his secret wish. The entire class listened intently – no one moved or made a sound, and most important, nobody laughed at him.

After that, things were a little different around the school for Steven. The other kids marveled at how brave he was for going over to that spooky house, and they realized that underneath those mismatched clothes, he was a pretty cool kid. So all because of a magic cookie, everyone lived happily ever after.

The End.

"NO!" the girls shouted.

"What about Grama and Pip?" Mandy whined.

"What about them" I asked, closing the book. "Did they get their wishes?" Cassy spoke up.

"Well, of course they did – I think. Let's take a look," I said opening the book back up.

"Yes, here it is!"

Every day after school, Mikel and Steven would visit Grandma Grama Kashuesta, just as they promised, and just like she wished. It was a friendship nothing could break, and they grew to love her like a real grandmother.

Now Pip-- poor Pip—he could never go back in time to be young, but he desperately wanted to see Kinwell again. Kinwell and his owners had only been here for a winter a long time ago. His owners were the visiting relatives of the family next door, and so when the visit was over, so was the friendship. Kinwell had to move back to South Carolina, because that is where he lived. Unfortunately, those relatives never came back to Littleton, and because Pip couldn't write letters (he is a cat), and he didn't know how to use the phone (again, he is a cat), he never spoke to Kinwell again.

"Aunt Warwee, that's just so sad," Mandy sniffled.

"Well, like I said, it was December, and what happens in December?"

"You never said it was December!" Mandy frowned.

"Guess what? It was December. Now, what happens in December?"

"Mom's birthday!" they shouted.

"What else happens in December?" I asked with great enthusiasm.

"It snows," Cassy cheered.

"Advent?" Mandy asked.

"NO! What happens on the 25th of December?" I closed my eyes, praying they could grasp the answer.

"Oh!" they laughed. "Christmas!"

Yes, and do you know what Grama did for Pip on Christmas? Well, she talked the neighbors into having Kinwell and his family up for the holidays and they agreed. So, on Christmas day, while Pip was watching Steven and Mikel play with their new toys – Steven in his new, matching snow suit and Mikel void glasses—a small knock came on the back door. Pip, thinking nothing of it, stayed at his perch on the windowsill, until Grama called him to the kitchen for some warm milk. What to his wondering eyes did appear, but Kinwell, his long ago friend. Well, Pip was so excited he did a little dance for joy, and then everyone lived happily ever after. THE END!

"I didn't know cats could dance, Aunt Warwee." Mandy questioned stretching her arms.

"Well this one could!" I slammed the book shut.

"Could he square dance or ballet dance?" she asked.

"I don't know – maybe. Get off my lap!"

Cassy took the book from my hands, "Do you think there are any stories in here about peanut butter sandwiches? I'm getting hungry."

The End.

Our Country Christmas Tree

Barbie-Jo Smith

It was Saturday, two weeks before Christmas and parents, Pete and Jane were enjoying a cup of coffee. Pete had found an advertisement from the newspaper featuring Christmas trees for $2.00 each. All you had to do was drive to the country and cut them. Pretty easy stuff he concluded. Several cups of strong coffee made the idea seem irresistible to him, however Jane heard alarm bells going off in her head. Peter reported that it was time they experienced the wonder of going for their own tree and besides wouldn't it be lots of fun to go out for a relaxing family day in the country. The children, Michael and Michelle needed to learn that the Yuletide tree didn't necessarily have to come from a box or from the Cub and Scout lot. The price was great and anyway, how hard could it be? More alarm bells. He rationalized that because their living room ceiling was slanted and 12 feet high at the top end, a nice big scotch pine would be wonderful snuggled into one of the corners. There was obviously no way that Jane could dissuade Pete from his quest, so she quietly suggested that he take the children and the dog and have a nice day. She would keep the home fires burning and have a nice warm stew waiting for them on their return. Jane was a very smart woman!

The advertisement said there would be a bonfire burning if people wanted to bring hot chocolate and wieners to make it a wonderful Yuletide family experience. Just drive northwest out of the city, turn on the gravel road and follow the signs. It was only "about ½ hour" drive. Knowing that Pete's talents did not include planning, Jane ensured that her children were properly dressed in snowsuits, with boots, mittens, hats and scarves. The dog, Star wagged her tail in anticipation so a quick executive decision was made. The travel group became one adult, two children and one hairy dog.

Meanwhile the limit of Pete's planning was to throw rope into the trunk of the car. One rope was good and two ropes were better. He had an idea that he would cut down a tree for their good friends, Stan and Wendy, who had a young family just like them. They would be so surprised and delighted. This is really going to be fun!

Although the family had two cars, one a large station wagon, Pete chose to take the small compact car. He calculated their gas savings with glee. A $2.00 Christmas tree and good gas mileage. Of course he forgot that the roof rack was on the big car and also the size of the car to size of the trees ratio. Well at least he had lots of rope. It never occurred to him to check the weather or depth of snow. The little car steamed northward and exited on the gravel road as planned. There were other cars headed in the same direction, so Pete just followed along. The road became progressively rougher as they advanced and they had to slow down to cross some sunken culverts presently they crossed the last culvert, dodged some rather large holes in the frozen gravel and drove in to a meadow. The bonfire was blazing cheerily and cars were parked to the sides. What a beautiful place. There were hills and valleys just filled with trees from which to choose.

They decided to split up and go in different directions to scout out the best trees. Michelle took Star on her leash, Michael went off on another trail and Pete headed forward. Of course the minimal planning phase didn't include proper clothing for Pete. He stepped off the parking lot into foot deep snow. He was wearing running shoes, jeans, short bomber jacket and ancient ski mittens. He didn't have a hat and carried only a hatchet, having forgotten the saw at home.

Eventually they found three suitable trees, agreed on one and Pete went to work while the children played with the dog. It wasn't a Scotch pine, but it was a really nice, tall tree with lots of branches and good shape. Because the branches were growing all the way to the ground, Pete had first clear away a lot of snow to get access to the trunk. Then he knelt down in the snow to begin hacking. He muttered to himself that he should have brought the saw but this was all he had and weren't they all having fun in the country.

The children were completely ignoring him and having a wonderful time rolling and playing in the snow with each other and the dog. The dog was in heaven as she bounded around plunging her head into the soft snow and then jumping out again. Every once in a while she had to stop and lay down to nibble the ice chunks out from between her toes. They she was at it again. They were having a grand time.

Meanwhile Pete was now laying on his side with the snow melting on his bare back as the bomber jacket slipped up. It didn't take long for his jeans to get damp and of course his feet had long since lost their feeling. He felt as if he had two blocks of wood on the ends of his shins. He realized he was very cold, however persevered and managed to cut through the trunk. With a call of timber, the tree sank onto its side.

Because Pete was so cold the tree for their friends, was chosen quickly. It wasn't quite as regal as the one they had chosen for themselves but it was acceptable and would fit in Stan and Wendy's living room. There were some bare spots but Pete rationalized that a few extra strands of tinsel would quickly fix up that problem. In no time he had the second tree cut and realized the downside of the beautiful hills. He manhandled the trees through several hills and valleys, and eventually back to the car. The children and dog frolicked beside him. They were are warm a toast and oblivious to their father's predicament. Pete thought how good hot chocolate and hot dogs would taste and with a sinking feeling remembered exactly where they were – at home on the counter. With a resigned sigh, he stumped forward on his block-like feet.

Pete loaded the kids in the car followed by Star whose coat was puffed out from snow between the hairs. As the car warmed up, the snow melted and the smell was akin to having a wet sheep in the vicinity. Pete looked at the size of the trees. They seemed small growing in the forest, but here beside the car, there were huge. Thank goodness he threw in an extra pile of rope. He knew there would be some lashing to the car, but he really did himself proud that day. He cracked the windows of the car, placed the trees on the car roof. Thank goodness he checked before tying them down because they were so long they completely covered the windshield. So Peter reversed one of them making a sight line. He then lashed them to the car by running the ropes through the car and around the trees. With other ropes he tied off the front and rear bumpers. Then he crawled into the car through the window, started the engine and turned the heat up full blast. He then knew that particular agony when one's toes are warming up from being so cold, but oh, the heat in the car felt so good. Steam began to rise as his clothing unthawed and they were quite a sight as they prepared to leave.

Pete was prudent as they left the parking lot and proceeded over the first sunken culvert. There was absolutely no load shift so all was very well to make the drive along the gravel road to the pavement. The drive home was uneventful, except for the rising steam and smell like they were all in a sheep shearing shed!

When they arrived home the children ran to their mother, dog close behind, to tell her about all the fun they had. Dad must have had fun too because he was laying in the snow playing with the hatchet and the tree! Pete untied the trees and chugged up the sidewalk, depositing them on the back deck. It was time to have a hot cup of coffee and change into dry clothes while his feet thawed. While Pete and the kids had been away, Jane rearranged the living room to make room for the tree in the corner. Having thawed sufficiently to walk, Pete dragged their tree into the living room and in short order discovered that it was enormous, even with the high ceiling. He laid it down and cut about 2 feet off the bottom to fit it into the corner. This time the job was done with a saw. As Pete sawed away in the living room, Jane and the kids disappeared into the bowels of the basement to retrieve boxes of Christmas decorations.

Having shortened the tree to fit, Pete wrestled it into the tree stand to let it thaw, congratulating himself on such a grand fine. He was especially happy that the tree was so fresh and wouldn't drop many needles because of that and the fact that any loose needles were blown off during the drive home. Jane's delicious warm stew was served for supper and the whole family dug in as if they hadn't eaten for days. This was close to the truth because of the forgotten hot dogs.

After supper when the tree had thawed and relaxed, it had to be positioned into the corner to camouflage the flaws. There were several gaping holes. As the children planned the decorating, Pete put the bulbs in miles of light strings. As lights were at that time, if one bulb was not working, the whole string didn't work, therefore the light check could take ages. However, having patched everything together, Pete next job was to deposit the lights on the top two thirds of the tree, followed by the angel at the top. He was the tall member of the family so the job naturally fell to him. As well, it's a time honored tradition that the father of the family strings the lights, plugging them in for the first time to make sure they're safe. If they're not, then he's subsequently blown off the ladder. It was thought that the tallest and strongest person in the family should have this job in order to survive the possible short circuits. With only a 6-foot ladder, Pete stretched to his full height to place the angel on the top. Then he threw the switch and the tree lit up with wonderful color. The entire family stepped back to adore the beautiful scene. No time to waste, the children were hard at it putting decorations on the tree, especially into the bare spots. One bare spot might house a dozen ornaments and a pound of tinsel. First came the ornaments which were pulled out with awe as everyone remembered them from the year before. Then came the garland and finally the tinsel. Finally, the coup de grace – candy canes. The children deposited them at a height they could easily reach if there was a candy emergency, but not low enough for the dog to reach. Too many times they had dealt with a dog that had intestinal difficulties at this time of year. When they finally realized that the dog was helping herself to candy and moved it higher on the tree, the mystery illness disappeared.

After reaching all the high spots Pete relaxed on the sofa to watch, a glass of Christmas cheer in his hand. All was right with his world. Despite a few hitches, the sojourn to the country to give the children a real country Christmas tree had gone surprisingly well. The feeling was returning to his feet and he had all his fingers. It had been a good adventure.

A few days later Stan and Wendy stopped by and were apprized that their $2.00 tree was waiting for them on the deck. One look at the tree and then their faces revealed that this poor tree with all the gaps and gouges was not quite suitable and they tactfully mentioned that they had already bought a tree. The second tree spent the Christmas season propped up on the deck in a way that it actually looked like it was growing there.

After the Christmas break, the children returned to school and Pete returned to work. The tree remained in the house until mid-January when it was decided that everyone was sick of looking at it. The Christmas season was definitely over. It was time to take it down and pack away the ornaments. The kids, having completely lost interest, promptly disappeared. Jane and Pete packed away the ornaments, tinsel, garland and several pounds of candy canes. Pete grappled with the tree and fought his way out the door and literally threw it on the snow. He had long ago learned to drag the tree out backwards, having been unceremoniously impaled the first time he removed a real tree. Used trees could be taken to the local fire hall for disposal. This time Pete tied the tree to the roof rack on the big car. He also threw on the gift tree which by now was just a bare pole surrounded by a circular pile of needles. There was a huge pile of trees at the fire hall, some of which still had the decorations and light strings on them. This was no doubt a testament from other young fathers who had faced the reality of cutting their own trees.

One Saturday in August of that year, Jane and Pete sat over morning coffee reminiscing about Christmas and how much fun it was to have a real tree. Wasn't it beautiful and it really wasn't that hard – was it? Shortly after that they went to a hardware sale and bought a tree in a box.

A Sweetwater ChrisMoose Story

by Sue A. Veryser

Part I
December 1994

Fog covered the tarmac at Metro Airport. Suddenly, in the quite unsuspecting town of Sweetwater, a moose appeared. Who was this moose and what was his purpose here?

Despite desperate attempts, by the Mayor, to make the town of Sweetwater a money Mecca, the big wigs would not cooperate. The Harbor issue had been OK'd and the stymied again. It was the one project that could bring money into the dying town, but alas, it appeared that it would never happen. Sweetwater was dying fast.

Businesses couldn't stay in business because no one ever came to town anymore. People would drive past it, but never through it. It was painfully clear that Sweetwater would never be anything more than a "sneeze, you miss it town." All the residents thought so, except for one.

T'was he who is him... they call him Tim. Tim was a barber and had been a barber in this town for the majority of his natural life. His father was a barber before him who is Tim. It was a family thing. But even the barber shop was beginning to fail.

December 23, 1994

The tree located in the middle of town had no lights. There were no ornaments or decorations to be found in or on any of the businesses and the manger at the Fire Hall never made its way out of storage. It looked to be a sad Christmas.

The quietly falling snow turned noisy, as the storm turned into a blizzard. Tim was on his way out for the night. As he locked the barbershop door behind him, he had the feeling that someone was watching him. Tim was a very brave man, but he was very apprehensive as he turned to face the street.

Nothing. The snow obscured everything in sight.
Tim walked around the corner to his mini-van, with the snow whipping about his feet. Still feeling like he was being watched, Tim reached his van with a sigh of relief. Suddenly, there was a giant gust of wind, and the snow mixed with ice whizzed about him, stinging every exposed part of his body. As Tim attempted to get the key in the frozen lock, a figure began to form in the depths of the snow and ice. Turning to face the street again, staring wide-eyed with disbelief, Tim dropped his keys.

Scrambling to retrieve them from the snow bank, he felt a warm breath on his neck. Slowly standing, Tim found himself face to face with a moose.

Tim looked at the moose, the moose looked at him.

"Hi, my name is Chris," the moose said.

"Uhhh...Mine's Tim."

"Don't be frightened, I'm here to help. That's what us Magic Moose do."

"Help who?" Tim stuttered.

"The town, you dope," the moose responded.

"You're the only one who has any hope for this place. So, together, we're going to open some eyes."

The snow and wind died down and all was quiet. Tim heard footsteps coming from behind him. It was Mike. Mike was the other barber that worked with Tim.

"Hey... what's happinin'? Who are you talking to?"
Tim spun around to face Mike, "The moose!" Tim exclaimed.

"What moose?"

"Are you blind? The moose that's standing behind me!"

"The moose that's standing behind you...OK..."

"He's right...," Tim pointed and looked in the direction of his finger, "there...Hey! Moose! Where'd ya go? He was right here. His name was Chris."

"Was it now...Chris Moose? Uh huh...go home Tim, it's been a long day."

Mike patted Tim on the shoulder and walked past him. "Really," Tim shouted to Mike, "I'm not seeing things!" Mike waved over his shoulder at Tim and kept walking. Tim stood by his van for quite some time before he finally decided that he should just stop at the local watering hole and try to gather his thoughts about what had just happened before going home. Maybe someone there would believe him.

Tim took his regular seat near the pool table and ordered a beer. Mike, Jay, Bob and Dale showed up soon after and took their seats at Tim's table. Mike, of course, was still shaking his head and laughing at Tim and had just begun to tell everyone else what Tim said he had seen when suddenly Tim jumped to his feet and stared toward the door.

"Mike! There he is!" Tim exclaimed pointing at the door. Now the rest of the people in the bar were staring, but they were all looking at Tim. Tim turned to face his friends at the table.

"Don't you see him? The Moose, Chris, he's big and standing by the door..."

"This is what I was just starting to tell you guys about," Mike mumbled to the rest of the table. "I think Tim needs a vacation."

"What is he looking at?" Bob asked.

"He thinks there is this magical moose named Chris standing at the door." Mike responded.

"That's kind of weird," Jay said. "Don't cha think?"

"Yeah, real weird," Dale said.

Through their conversation, Tim had gotten up and walked over to the door. He stood there talking to, what appeared to everyone else to be, air. "Hey, how come no one else can see you Chris?" Tim asked.

"They're not supposed to. You're the chosen one."

"What's with this chosen crap? Who chose me?"

"You did," Chris responded.

"I did...how exactly did I do this?"

"You're the only one left in this town with any love or hope for it. I already told you that. Tim, the town needs your help, but, that choice is yours."

"Great! All my friends think I'm insane. What am I supposed to do? Just tell me what to do, so my life will go back to normal. I can't live this way."

"Well," Chris said, "It's really quite simple. This town is dying because there is no spirit here, Christmas or otherwise. You must help me instill the Christmas Spirit before midnight, Christmas Eve or there will be no hope for this town. It will crumble and fall and become a giant parking lot."

"A parking lot aye? Hmmmm...can I have time to think about this? I mean, how do I know you're even real? I could have just eaten something bad, or I could be dreaming right now...I don't know. I need some time. Who sent you anyway?"

Chris stared into Tim's eyes. "Someone pretty big. Don't take too much time Tim. We don't have much to waste."

"Yeah...OK...we'll talk...another time. You're embarrassing me."

The moose disappeared and Tim walked back to his table and took his seat. Of course, everyone was still staring and whispering about how weird Tim was acting. Tim finished his beer without another word to anyone, got up and walked to the door.

"Hey Tim, where are you going buddy?" Mike asked.

"Maybe I should give you a lift home."

Tim just opened the door, shook his head and walked out. It was late and the snow had started again. The drive home was silent.

Tim crawled into bed and snuggled up to his wife. It was good to be home. What a strange day. As Tim began to settle in and fall asleep, he heard a loud crash. It sounded like it came from the kitchen.

Tim jumped to his feet and slowly rounded the corner to the kitchen, after grabbing a broom from the hallway, of course. There, standing with his head in the refrigerator and a jar of grape jelly stuck to his nose, was none other than Chris.

"What the hell are you doing here?" Tim shouted. "I thought you were going to give me time to think. Don't you have someone else to visit?"

"I changed my mind and I was hungry." Chris answered.

"Besides, I know if I give you too much time, you won't help."

"I thought you said it was my choice..."

"Dear...who are you yelling at?" That was his wife's voice. Tim hadn't realized that he had been shouting.

"Uhhh... I'm talking to myself." Yeah, that sounded good, Tim thought. But what was worse, talking to a magic moose or to himself?

"All right! I'll do what you say. Just hurry before my wife comes in here," Tim whispered.

"Get your coat and get on my back," Chris said.

"Get on your back...where are we going?"

"You'll see."

So, on Chris's back Tim did climb and in the twinkling of an eye, they were outside the house and airborne.

"You can fly...but I'm afraid of heights."
"Just hang on Tim; this will only take a minute."

"Couldn't we just walk?"

"This is much faster. Remember, I'm a magical moose.

There are a lot of things I can do and you're going to have to learn to trust me now."

"I really don't have much of a choice now, do I?"

Through the air Tim and Chris flew. Over the rooftops and mountain peaks they glided. They were both silent.
Moments later...

"Hold on Tim, we've reached our destination and were going in for a landing. Sometimes my landings are a little rough." Chris laughed.

"Rough!"

Tim looked down and below them was a tiny little town that looked a lot like Sweetwater, and right in the center was a small little shop all aglow. As they got closer to the ground and were ready to land, Tim thought he saw a man that looked a lot like what Santa Claus was thought to look like, but how could that be? Was there really a Santa Claus?

"Hey! Positive thoughts there Timmy!" Chris shouted back to him. There were on the ground now.

"Nice landing Chris, what was all that about, positive thoughts?"

"You were doubting Santa Claus." Chris answered.

"How did you know that? What...can you read my thoughts too?"

Chris didn't answer; he was standing at the door of the little shop. Chris motioned for Tim to get down. Tim jumped off and peered through the door. Tiny people hurried here and there, wrapping presents and loading them into big burlap bags. There were Christmas lights and trees everywhere and right in the middle of all the commotion was indeed, Santa himself.

"Hey Chris! That really is Santa Claus! Now what do I do?"
"Go tell him what the problem is in your town."
So Tim told Santa of Sweetwater's problems and Santa of course, agreed to help. They climbed aboard the sleigh; with

Chris Moose leading the team of reindeer and off they went.

Upon their arrival in Sweetwater, Santa saw what Tim had described to him and was saddened by the lack of spirit and love in the hearts of the town folk. It was worse than what he had envisioned.

"It was good of Chris to pick you to help this town and it was smart of him to bring you to me. I'll do my best to help." Santa patted Tim on the head. (Tim was a little man).

Santa parked behind the barber shop and he, Chris and Tim went inside. Mike was cutting the Chief of Police's hair and almost buzzed him when he saw Tim, Santa and the moose standing in the doorway.

"Tim...there's...there's a moose next to you and a guy that looks like Santa?" Mike was stuttering he couldn't believe his eyes.

As Mike was speaking, a crowd began to form outside. Hundreds of town folk had seen the sleigh in the sky above the town and had come running to see if it was real.
Santa turned to face the crowd, as did Chris. The crowd gasped. There really is a Santa Claus and he was right there in their town.

Santa didn't have to say a word. The crowd dispersed and

frantically began to decorate. Carols were being sung, the tree began to glow and the Spirit of Christmas was renewed in the town of Sweetwater that day.

Tim had done it. He was a hero in the minds of all the town folk.

Christmas came and went in all of its glory and right after the tree came down in January, a statue of Tim riding the Magic Moose was erected in the middle of the town so everyone would remember how special Christmas really was to the whole world.

The town actually prospered after that season. Construction of the harbor began that spring and people actually started driving through Sweetwater again, which helped the businesses immensely.

And rumor has it, that on foggy nights, down at the harbor, a moose can be seen flying through the air.

Part II
December, 1996

Two years had passed since that magical Christmas. The town hasn't changed at all. The statue of Tim riding the Magical Moose stands tall in the middle of town and in front of it, is the town's Christmas tree.

Sweetwater had certainly learned its lesson, for as far as the eye could see, Christmas was everywhere. There wasn't a tree un-decorated, a building without a wreath, a street lamp without a lighted angel or a person without a smile on their face or a kind work on their lips. It was indeed a Christmas Season un-surpassed by any other.

December 23, 1996 ~ 6:00 p.m.

Normy was walking across the street in front of the tree, when suddenly; a big gust of wind blew his stocking cap off his head. Scrambling to retrieve the hat that was being shuffled across the street, Normy failed to look both ways before crossing. Jay, who was in route around the tree to get to the barber shop, slammed on his brakes, and swerved to avoid Normy, but couldn't avoid accidently hitting John (Mr. Fixit) who was carelessly riding his bike in front of the tree.

Upon impact, John was launched; bike and all, into the

tree and the chain reaction began. The tree started to wobble, pulling itself free from its restraints with each slow teeter. The more John fought to get himself un-stuck from the branches, the more the tree swayed until suddenly, without much warning, the tree came crashing down right smack dab into the middle of the barber shop across the street.

Jay still swerving to avoid the tree, managed to miss it only to hit the statue on the other side, smashing it to smithereens.

Suddenly, the town fell silent. People from all over the city town came running to see what all the commotion was about and upon arriving on the scene, sadness filled their hearts and the Christmas Spirit slowly melted away.

Climbing out of the rubble, Tim and Mike stood on the sidewalk. Thankful that they were already closed for the day, but furious at the sight of the Christmas Tree lodged in the middle of the shop, Tim threw his hands in the air (not literally) and angrily announced his retirement.

"You can't quit!" Mike exclaimed.

"What?" Tim asked, "I can't hear you over Holly's screaming."

Holly lived in the apartment above the barber shop and had been sitting quietly on the couch when the tree fell through the window and knocked her off her seat, out the window, and onto the canopy located just above the shop.

"I said, "Mike shouted, "You can't quit! Holly, be quiet, we'll get you down. Somebody call the fire department." Mike shouted over his shoulder.

"Sure I can," Tim answered, "I'm too old for this crap! I'll pick my stuff up in the morning and I'm moving to Las Vegas."

"Tim, you can't," Mike pleaded, "this town needs you, especially now. Look at 'em all. These people are depending on you. And now, with the statue destroyed and the tree gone, they're going to need you more than ever to find the spirit again. Remember what Chris Moose told you? You're the Ch..."

"Listen Mike, I don't care what that silly moose said two years ago. I've done my job. I've paid my dues. Look at my shop! Tell me you wouldn't do the same. Tell me you wouldn't walk away!"

"Well, at least sleep on it, "Mike argued back. "Don't make a decision you'll regret."

Tim grumbled, walked to his Explorer and drove away, leaving Mike in the middle of a large crowd of depressed people.
The fire department, police, and the city workers arrived on the scene and proceeded to get Holly down from the canopy, John and his bike out of the tree, and began cleaning up the mess. There was no way to fix the tree or to get a new one erected by Christmas, and as far as the barber shop went, well, there was no fixing that either, not quickly anyway. The remains of the statue of Chris Moose and Tim were swept up and carted away.

By 9:00 p.m., the town was silent. The carols heard earlier had ceased. The town folk refused to turn on their Christmas lights, and the businesses shut down early for the night without so much as a friendly smile or a how do you do.

It doesn't take much to destroy the Spirit, when trouble hovers over a whole town. Something as simple as kindness can be quickly wiped away, when hopelessness finds a way to consume the human spirit.

Tim laid on his couch in front of the fireplace. His wife and daughter were across town at a friend's Christmas party, but Tim just wasn't in the mood for Christmas anymore. Instead, he just laid there, staring off into the fire, filled with the "self-pity and poor me" syndrome. He slowly drifted off to sleep.

In the meantime, Mike had quickly rushed home to call the North Pole. He needed to get Chris Moose here right away. There was only one day left before Christmas, and unlike most of the town folk, Mike knew the consequences for lack of Christmas Spirit. He knew what would happen to Sweetwater if he failed to convince Tim to stay. Other than Tim, only Mike knew of Tim's destiny and unfortunately, Tim didn't seem to care about it anymore.

You see, two years ago, Chris Moose had given Tim a very special gift. Tim held it very close, knowing he was very fortunate to have been picked out of an entire world full of people to have the power of the Christmas Spirit with him all year. He also knew that the spirit could be defeated very easily, and if he lost that spirit, it would not just be Sweetwater that would be in trouble, but the entire world.

Every 100 years, a new Keeper of the Spirit is picked. His job is to keep the Christmas Spirit safe within himself, to spread it to everyone he meets, and to keep it away from the despair that surrounds the world. Tim had that honor bestowed upon him two years ago and until today, he had proven to be worthy, but somehow, despair had found its way in and there was only one who could help stop it from spreading, only one who could save Tim.

"Chris, it's Mike. Listen, we're in serious trouble here. Tim wants to quit the barber shop, close it up, and retire. He wants to move to Vegas and forget about everything. See..." Mike told Chris the whole story of the tree, the statue being destroyed and the barber shop damage; you know the whole kin-n-caboodle. Chris listened closely and told Mike to sit tight. He was on his way.

Sleepily, Tim rolled over on the couch and pulled the covers up around his neck. It was getting cold in the house. The fireplace needed another log, but he didn't feel like getting up to do it. Closing his eyes again, Tim began to drift back to sleep, but he couldn't shake the feeling that he was being watched. Slowly,

Tim opened one eye and suddenly, SLURP! A giant lounge licked his face.

"What the..!" Tim exclaimed and jumped up from the couch. And there standing in front of him was his old friend Chris.

"What are you doing here? Let me guess, Mike called you in to save the day, right? You're here to talk me out of leaving Sweetwater. You're here to convince me that I'm making a mistake. That the people in Sweetwater need me, all that baloney, right?" Tim stopped, realizing he was ranting and probably looked like a mad man.

Chris just stood, saddened by his friend's change of heart. Both were silent for a long time. Finally, Tim spoke.

"I'm sorry Chris. It's just that, Christmas is a day away and now everything looks so bleak. The shop that my Grandfather established is in rubble. I don't have the kind of money to restore it. You know the insurance company isn't going to cover all of it. They never do. So, here I sit, I know, feeling sorry for myself, but I just can't shake it."

"Tim," Chris said softly, "do you remember the gift I gave you two years ago?"

"Yeah!"

"Do you remember what I told you to do if you found despair setting in and covering the spirit in darkness?"

Tim nodded. Chris continued. "It's not just Sweetwater that's in trouble. The whole world needs you. It's a lot of pressure, but you would not have been chosen if we had doubted your integrity or ability. The Spirit still lies within you, not in the barber shop, not in the Christmas tree and certainly not in the silly statue. The Spirit really lies in all of us, but the people look to you for the guidance to find it within themselves. That's your job. The rewards are great Tim; I think you already know that."

Tim sat looking at the floor. He knew what Chris was saying was true and he knew he had little time to fix what he had destroyed.

Mike had thought of Tim not only as his best friend, but as somewhat of a Dad, since his own Dad had passed away five years ago. There was nothing he wouldn't do for the man. He hurried back to the barber shop and tried desperately to clean up the broken glass and dismantled chairs left in the wake of the fallen Christmas tree. He quickly carried and stacked the dislodged bricks into a nice pile alongside of the shop. If Chris showed up, he knew he would bring Tim here, and if Tim could see the shop a little less hairy, maybe it would help to erase some of the hopelessness that surround him.

It was almost midnight, when Mike had finished cleaning up as much as the debris as he could without help. Looking at the clock, Mike wondered about his friend. Would Chris be able to change his mind, change his heart in time? Mike plugged in the only string of lights left unbroken, turned on some country Christmas music and waited.

"Get on my back, Tim," Chris said. "Let's go spread that Spirit!"

"Ya' know...we're not that far away from the shop now. Couldn't we just walk it? I remember the last time we did this, I didn't get a kick out of it then, and I doubt I'll like it much better now. I just turned 50 and would like to see 51."

"Get up there," Chris motioned to his back. "Stop being such a wimp. This is much faster and you know it."
So, once again, on Chris's back, Tim did climb, and in the twinkling of an eye they were outside the house and airborne.

They arrived at the shop two seconds later, and Chris saw what had made Tim let despair inside. It was a mess and it would take a while to fix. Tim jumped down off of Chris's back. "See what I mean? It's destroyed...wait...hey, at least one string of Christmas lights still works. Check it out Chris. Pretty amazing aye?"

Chris said nothing.

"Do you hear Christmas music Chris?" Tim asked.

Chris nodded.

"Well what do you know about that? See, these people don't need me, they found the Spirit without me..."

Chris nudged Tim in the back with his nose, pushing him towards the gaping hole where the door used to be.

"Hey! OK, OK, I'm going. If you're trying to cheer me up, making me go back inside isn't going to help much, but I'm going. I'm going."

Tim slowly walked inside trying to adjust his eyes to see in the darkness. That one string of lights didn't give off a whole heck of a lot of light, but he managed to feel his way inside and was surprised to find that the shop was surprisingly clean. He moved towards the back of the shop and there sitting in his barber chair was Mike.

While Mike was home calling Chris Moose, he also called a few of Tim's friends and asked them to help him with fixing things up.

As Tim stood looking at Mike, a city truck pulled up alongside of the shop and in tow was a new tree. Mike knew a guy, Dale, who had wanted to donate a tree from his front yard for years, so he called in the request and Dale quickly cut it down.

The Fire Department guys showed up within minutes and before anyone could say "Bah Humbug," the tree was up and decorated.

From the back room of the shop Christmas music could be heard. The door flew open and there stood all of Tim's best friends. Dave, Bobby, Roy, Herbie, John, Butch, Bill, Doug, Joe and practically the whole rest of the town stood in the small shop all dressed in Santa hats and right in the middle stood none other than Santa Clause himself. Yeah, Mike called him too.

One by one, the town folk came out and crowded around the new tree. Then Chris spoke.

"Christmas is not about trees, lights, magic moose, Santa or statues. These are all just reminder of the real stuff that makes Christmas, Christmas. It's about human kindness, loving your neighbor, feeling that come from deep within you, family, friends, peace on Earth and goodwill toward all living things. It is the time of year when we are all a little kinder, a little happier, a little more generous, and more loving. Tim's job is to show the world that you can have all of this, all year round. It doesn't have to be a once a year thing. Even when things go bad for us, we must never lose the Spirit that we have within us. Right, Tim?"

Tim agreed. He had found the spirit again and was entrusted with its safety for the next 50 years (which would make him 100 years old at the time of retirement...).

Tim stood on one side of Chris and Mike stood on the other. The Christmas Spirit filled the town and it didn't have anything to do with a tree or statue, it had to do with friends, family and togetherness.

The following spring, the town finally filled in the hole where the statue of Tim and Chris once stood.

They didn't need a new statue of Tim, because they had the real thing right in front of them every day. And as far as Chris Moose goes, well, no one would ever forget him. (Who could forget a talking and flying moose?)

Mike was never quite the same, however, for he knew he had played a major role in helping his best friend. He never really gloated about it or anything, but whenever anyone brought up the story of that Christmas, Mike would get a funny smirk on his face and chuckle to himself.

As for Sweetwater, well, the story certainly doesn't end here.

Memories Of A
Charlie Brown Christmas

By David L. Brown

This is not about the Charles Schultz, Peanuts cartoon family. It's about the memories of the years from my family. My Dad 's name is Charlie Brown. Our family consists of seven kids, three boys and four girls and our parents. We are the typical family living in a two story house with a fenced in backyard. Upstairs in our house were bedrooms and a half bath. The boys had one bedroom and the girls had the others. As you go down the stairs and walk straight you would be in Mom and Dad's bedroom. Turn right and you will be I the living room, to the left was the bathroom. Attached to the living room was the kitchen, then the utility room between the kitchen and family room. Continue to the right from the family room and you are back to our parents' bedroom.

Christmas time the Christmas tree was always in the family room for good reasons. My older brother and I would always try to sneak a peek at the Christmas presents after everyone went to bed on Christmas Eve. There was always one problem; Dad would sleep on the couch in the living room. This meant we would have to sneak through their bedroom and open the door going into the family room or sneak past Dad. Neither option was easy.

One Christmas stands out in my mind regarding our late night sneaking. I had to be about ten years old and my brother thirteen. My brother was leading the way. There was Dad sleeping on the couch as we started to move nice and quiet, Dad stirred. I took off running and hid in the family room. My brother got busted in the kitchen. I could hear Dad telling him to get back to bed. That's when my brother ratted me out telling Dad if he had to go back to bed than so does Dave. My hiding spot was very good it took him some time before he found me. In a corner alcove of the family room Dad had built a bar with storage areas for our toys under it. Being small I could fit into one storage area and to hide I covered up with stuffed animals. Dad then escorted us to the stairs and watched as we went up as he said DO NOT come back down before seven.

It was about seven thirty when we finally woke up and headed down stairs. By then Mom was awake and we cut through the bedroom into the family room. Our ages ranged from thirteen down to a newborn if my math is correct. When we started to rip open our presents the wrapping paper was flying everywhere. The excitement level was unbelievable. As things settled down in the family room Dad yelled for me to come into the kitchen. When I walked into the kitchen you could see something covered by a blanket in the corner. By now everyone was in the kitchen as I pulled back the blanket. I think the whole neighborhood could have heard me scream as I stood there looking at a mini-bike. It was gold with a black seat and sissy bar I couldn't wait to take it outside and ride it. Dad handed me a helmet to wear while riding it. After my excitement settled down I wondered how I did not see that when I ran through earlier in the night.

As my brother and I got older we decided we would rather sleep than sneak down the stairs on Christmas Eve. This job was passed on to our younger brother when he was old enough to attempt it. There were two sisters between him and me and two sisters younger than he was. Only the second girl of the bunch was really interested in snooping. For some unknown reason our younger brother was the only one who never got caught. Come to think of it he is still sneaky to this day.

The Christmas memories continue to grow as our family grows. One of the funniest things we enjoyed was each time a new girlfriend or boyfriend was introduced to our family that was not used to a large family. Having seven kids in a family this repeated itself many times. The typical family gathering included all of our family; spouses, kids, boyfriends or girlfriends and grandparents. There was always a potluck style dinner before presents could be opened. It was held at Mom and Dad's house that I had described earlier. As time went on the family grew you can imagine how crowded our house was.

In 1977 prior to arriving at Mom and Dad's house I proposed to my girlfriend, and she said YES. When it was time to open presents we announced it to the family, everyone was excited for us. It was time for the opening and the paper began flying if you were lucky you might see some elbows in the midst of the paper. In the middle of all this excitement Dad leaned over and asked my new Fiancé, Debbie if she was still willing to go through with this? We all laughed. This was her first experience with my total family.

Every family has good and not so good memories from Christmas. 1978 was one of the not as good memories. This was the first Christmas for Deb and I as a married couple. We were up opening our gifts from each other when there was knocking at our apartment door. It was my aunt who lived across the courtyard from us in the apartment complex. Mom had called her to have her come and tell us my Grandmother past away earlier that morning on the way to church. This was my Dad's mother. We all tried to put on a happy face throughout the day but it was hard. We did have some laughs as we reminisced about the times with Grandma.

Through the years it seemed that someone would receive a gag gift. This year it we my little brother was in for a surprise. A couple of people had planned to get him a blow up doll and dress it up. Now neither of these devious people was me. What I will say that it took our brother in law and mother all afternoon to inflate that thing. After all the gifts were opened and everyone was sitting around talking our brother in law came walking in with the doll and handed to my brother. Laughter and teasing went on for quite a while.

Little brother is not the type to let a good deed go undone. After some prodding by everyone he decided to put the doll in the car of sister number two and her husband. She was at her in laws house prior to coming to Mom and Dad's. He took an accomplice with him and parked just down the road from the car. They snuck that doll into the back seat without being seen and came back to the house. These were the days when no one locked their cars. A short time later our sister and her husband came over to Mom and Dad's. They did not say a word about the doll. The two delivery boys had no idea what was going on as they knew it was in the right car. They couldn't take the suspense any longer and commented about finding something in their car. Both of them said there was nothing in their car that maybe whatever it was they put it in his brother's car which looked similar to theirs. His brother was seven feet tall and went well over two hundred fifty pounds. At this time there were two nervous people. After they let them sweat a while longer our brother in law went out and brought the doll in the house. The look of relief on two faces was priceless. Our family has its share of practical jokers especially at someone else's expense.

Christmas was a time when the whole family could be together.

As time marched on and the family continued to grow this was not the case with some having to work or had their own family commitments.   There was always a large group and with the smaller kids coming along the chaos grew. The older people had as much fun watching as the little kids did opening presents. It was always comical.

The year sister number one brought her new boyfriend home at Christmas was no exception. He was rather shy at first like most people when you meet the family. When dinner was over as usual it was time for the chaos to begin and open presents. All the small kids sat in the middle of the room on the floor chomping at the bit to start opening. The safest place to be is either in a doorway where you could step out or sitting away from the tree. Dad and I took our usual spots, he in his recliner and I on the end of the couch. The new guy being unsure what to expect stayed in a back corner out of the way. The gifts were handed out and the paper was flying everywhere you could hardly see the kids on the floor. I looked over at the boyfriend and he was just standing there with his mouth hanging opened in utter shock. Nudging Dad, I pointed him out both of us were laughing so hard we were crying. There is nothing like the introduction to a large family at Christmas. Even as the years have passed since that time I am still smiling as I write about it.

Up to this point we had always gathered at Mom and Dad's house for Christmas Eve. My older brother and his family had just moved back from Phoenix and had purchased a house with a nice full basement and wanted to host the gathering this year. Everyone agreed. Our brood filled the basement with all the gifts stacked in the corner taking up almost six feet out from the wall. It was normal chaos and everyone had a good time. It just didn't feel like Christmas not being at Mom and Dad's. The next year we went back to the scene of the original crime.

Each year brought new memories and added to all the good and not as good ones of the past. Over the years Grandparents, Aunts and Uncles have passed on. Some of us now we have grandkids. Unfortunately, some are not in the area. There are some in Phoenix and Denver. Technology does make it easier to communicate with them and let them see all of us. The memories of Christmas past are always reminisced and laughed at all the good times wishing those who are not there could be with us.

The year 2003 brought some of those not as good memories to Christmas. Dad was very ill and pretty much bed ridden under Hospice care. This would be his last Christmas with us. As you can imagine bringing the utter chaos into the house would not be good on Dad. Not to mention with the hospital bed in the living room there was not much room. Sister number three and her husband were gracious enough to host Christmas Eve gathering. They had a beautiful home and full finished basement with plenty of room. During the day on Christmas

Eve I think everyone came by Mom and Dad's to visit with them and spend time with Dad. The leader of humor for the family was Dad and I followed as a close second. Everyone always said I inherited his sense of humor (albeit sick at times). I still remember him talking about when he was diagnosed with cancer and bringing the family together to tell us. He looked over at me and said "You knew what you were doing that night didn't you? I said, "Yep, I would not ask a question in a time like that without knowing the answer. Dad said, "Yeah they wanted to kill you!" "But they all stopped crying didn't they?" I responded. We had a good laugh. Seeing him smile was the best gift I could have received. The question I asked, "Hey Pop, can I have your three wheeler?" His response, "Hell no I am taking it with me!" Dad had always said he bought an extra grave for all of his toys and he was taking them with him and no one was getting them.

That evening no one was in much of a mood to celebrate as you can imagine. We tried to keep a smile on for all the young kids to not upset them. We did share a lot of memories that evening with each other realizing how special each year was to all of us. Dad passed five days later.

The years since dad passed we have moved the Christmas Ever gathering to Sister number one and her husband's home just down the road from Moms. They love to entertain and when they built the house it was built with that in mind. There was plenty of room and the older of our kids would head to the basement to play pool or watch movies. That is until it was time to open gifts. We still have all of the food and eat until we are about to blow. There is so much less work on Mom having it at their house. Its' still not the same as having at Moms but it works and everyone has a good time.

What started out as Mom and Dad grew to seven kids then add seven spouses to the mix and as Mom tells us she has eighteen grandchildren and thirteen great-grandchildren. You can imagine even with a portion of the family there a lot of wrapping paper is flying. Mom still says we are making her old and not wanting to argue with our Mother we tell her yes she is.

When it was just my older brother and I Dad used to film Christmas and did a couple years after sister number one was born. On occasion I would get these out and watch them. Now the old eight millimeter films are so brittle we are afraid to touch them. This year to surprise all of my brothers and sisters not to mention Mother they are all getting put on a DVD along with the family vacation films showing a lot of the family that have passed away over the years.

In the early years when there wasn't so many of us everyone would buy a gift for everyone else. As the family grew we began drawing names for the adults and kids. This too became some families spending more than others. Now with all the grandchildren and great-grandchildren they young of which are those that receive gifts other than Mother who gets one from everyone. Which we still keep trying to talk her out of.

Our Christmas memories are forever in our hearts to remember and tell stories like this. Whenever we get together at this time of year in any number we always seem to reminisce of all the fun at Christmas. Always wondering what Dad would think of all these little great grandkids.

LAKEVIEW POWERSPORTS
We do Parts and Service Right

- PWC
- Boat Repairs
- Dirt Bikes
- Four Wheelers
- UTV's
- Snowmobile
- Oil Changes

We fix just about anything with a motor in it!

**32525 23 Mile Rd • Chesterfield Twp., MI. 48047 --
lakeviewpowersports.com**

586-725-5009

Lakeview Motel

**A Gem of a Motel, located on beautiful Anchor Bay in Fair Haven.
Owned and Operated by Gene and Pam Boyd for 19 years.**

**Rooms have queen beds, cable TV, small refrigerators, WiFi.
Two rooms overlook the Bay and have two queen beds each.
Small refrigerators, microwave, coffee pot.
Efficiency apartment when available.**

586-725-0551

The Christmas Closet

By Ashley Ann Allen

"Elaina, have you written your letter to Santa Claus yet?"

"Mama, I'm 8. Santa is for babies. You know I know it's you every year, right? Like, I've known since I was 5. Every Christmas Eve, when I go to bed, you sneak into the closet, remove my letter, and fill the shelves with the gifts I'd asked for. You totally read my letter as soon as I write it and buy everything."

"Elaina, I'm surprised at your lack of spirit this year. At least you usually play along. Come on now; Daddy and I were going to also write our letters, and then we can bake cookies."

"And then you'll leave some of the cookies in the Christmas Closet in a storage tin with our notes, just like you do every year. Even though it's not even Halloween. Sarah's parents don't make do this baby stuff, especially this early. It's like you're obsessed."

As soon as she said it, Elaina knew she'd hurt mama's feelings. Still, with the stubbornness of youth, she uttered no apology. Instead, she followed mama into the kitchen and sat at the dining table. After selecting a drab brown piece of construction paper and a basic black marker, she wrote her obligatory letter to Santa.

Dear Santa,
For Christmas this year, I want money and lots of it. See, I know you aren't real and that mama and daddy buy my gifts, so I'm gonna cut out the middle man. I'll save the money and spend it on stuff I want later, like that awesome new Monster High doll that Sarah has that mama said was too expensive. If that's too much to ask, then just get me some socks or something. I don't really care that much. I'm just writing this letter cause mama wants me to.
Signed,
Elaina.

Following their usual ritual, Elaina helped mama bake and decorate Christmas cookies that cool October evening. She carried the tin full of cookies and the family's letters to the empty closet in the hall, the one her parents dubbed the Christmas Closet.

Elaina awoke early for no discernible reason one crisp December morning. She looked at the clock on the bedside table. 05:03 it read, the red digital letters almost glaring at her in the otherwise dark bedroom. She could hear mama getting ready to head to work.

Daddy will probably sleep in since I'm out of school for Christmas, she thought.

She knew she could slip her Minnie Mouse house shoes on and be at the door to hug mama goodbye, but the patchwork quilt grandma had made for Christmas a few years back was super warm, and she'd see mama later that day.

Best to try and go back to sleep.

~~~

Daddy called Elaina in from the yard. He looked very upset.

"Whatever it is, I didn't do it!" she blurted, searching her brain for some mischievous action she must've committed recently.

"Elaina...we need to go to the hospital."

"But, why? I'm not sick. Are you sick? Should I call 911?!"

"No, Elaina...it's mama. There's been an accident."

~~~

Elaina cried the whole way to the hospital. When she and daddy arrived, a doctor pulled daddy aside and spoke to him in hushed tones. Daddy burst into loud sobs, something Elaina had never before seen him do, and that's when she knew.

~~~

Christmas morning was unbearable for Elaina and daddy. Elaina had yanked open the closet door, only to find the cookies and letters still there. She knew it would be that way. Mama was the magic of the Christmas Closet, not some dumb old Santa. And with mama gone, Christmas was gone.

All daddy had done since that day at the hospital was cry. Daddy was never a crier before. Elaina couldn't bear to see it, but when grandma had tried to convince daddy to let her take Elaina for a while, both daddy and Elaina said no. Elaina didn't want to leave daddy and this house. It was all she had left of mama. Elaina cried herself to sleep Christmas night, that year and every year.

~~~

Elaina wasn't sure why she was bothering driving home to see daddy in the middle of October. She was at her dream college only a few hours from home, but far enough away to be herself. Why did she keep up this stupid Christmas tradition with daddy, year after year?

She'd tolerated writing letters to Santa all the way through high school, but had told herself she wouldn't do it once she left home.

Every Christmas morning, just like it had been the year mama died, the closet was devoid of anything Christmas except those cookies and letters. It was heartbreaking. Why didn't daddy just buy one or two gifts and fill the closet up like mama used to do, even if it wasn't everything on their lists? Why did he insist on keeping up this charade, painfully?

~~~

It snowed on Christmas Eve that year. Elaina and daddy made a snow family. They made mama into an angel.   Elaina went to bed in her old room that night, bracing herself mentally for the annual disappointment that would be Christmas morning.

She pleaded with the stars she could see out the window--please let daddy just put a gift in there, just one gift. She knew he didn't even read the letters, so if he put something in there, she'd pretend it was the one thing she'd always wanted, even if it was socks.

When Elaina awoke, she could hear daddy downstairs making coffee. For a moment, she contemplated just sleeping in. Then she realized that opening the closet made daddy happy, in a weird way, even though the closet remained empty, year after year.

She put on her robe over her PJs, slipped into her house slippers, a subdued pink design, and padded downstairs to make her own cup of coffee.

Daddy already had a cup waiting for her, two creams, one sugar, just the way she liked it.

"Let's go!" he said, with unnecessary enthusiasm.
Elaina followed him groggily to the closet.

"You do the honors, Elaina." daddy smiled.

"Okay, but brace yourself for the avalanche!" she said, sarcastically.

It was the same joke that mama used to make, but neither of them had uttered it since mama died.

When Elaina opened the closet, there was indeed an avalanche. Gift upon gift poured out of the Christmas closet. To: Elaina From: Santa read many of the packages. Others read To: Daddy From: Santa which is what they'd always said when mama had opened the closet for them every Christmas morning.

Though Elaina was sure this was daddy's doing, he appeared just as shocked as she was.

Carefully, they picked up each of the gifts and divided them into their respective piles in the living room.

When Elaina opened the first gift, there was a pack of socks. Elaina laughed emotively. The second gift was large; it turned out to be the Monster High doll like she'd wanted as a kid.

Each gift she opened was something she'd written on her

letters to Santa, letters daddy had never opened in front of her and she hadn't seen since.

Daddy seemed surprised at his own pile of loot: a box of golf balls, a copy of Moby Dick in a faux leather binding, a new shaving kit...each box they opened was one more materialistic thing they'd hastily scrawled each year, while each telling themselves that nothing would be in the closet and that what they really wanted was mama back.

Elaina and daddy hugged and giggled that day, and, for the first Christmas morning in a decade, they felt like mama was with them.

Monkey's First Christmas

By Laura T'rese Veryser

Not too long ago in the land of New Baltimore...

"What happened to the old Baltimore?" Mandy asked, pushing me back onto the couch – Seems it was bigger than the old red chair we use to gather in to read our stories from the cookbook together, and consequently they were bigger, too—older and taller, that is.

"It is in Maryland," I said adjusting under the weight of their leaning.

"They moved the entire city all the way to Michigan?" Krista was astounded.

"No, just the name," I replied.

"Oh, why not call it the Other Baltimore?" she put her head on my shoulder.

"Shhhh!" I shushed her, "Listen."

When the month of October had arrived and the autumn winds began to make its entrance by bullying all the leaves off the tree—there was a wee black and white spotted kitten born

113

in a small apartment with four other black and white spotted kittens.

"I thought this was a Christmas story," Cassy interrupted.

"It is," I answered.

"Christmas is in December," Cassy said, throwing her leg over mine.

I threw her leg off of mine, "Don't interrupt me so much during this story!"

This wee kitten stayed snuggled close to her mom and siblings (brothers and sisters) until the holiday season had arrived.

"Now, let me see if I understand this—was it a little kitten or did is say WEE instead of meowing?" Markie asked from his spot on the back of the couch.

One afternoon, late in November, when the "little" kitten was a little bigger, a dad stranger came to the little apartment with a little girl stranger. While the little girl stranger was playing with all the kittens, the owner of the apartment and the dad stranger talked business, and soon the little kitten's oldest brother disappeared out the door with the stranger dad and the little girl stranger. The little kitten wasn't worried though.

One time her mom went out the door and came back in again, so she continued to play with her other brother and two older sisters, waiting for her brother's return.

Many naps have past, and he still wasn't back. The little kitten started to worry about him so much, that she could only take eleven naps a day – which is unusual for a kitten. The kitten's mother noticed this and decided to talk to all the kittens.

"Last year it was a dancing cat – now they talk?" Michael frowned at me.

"Only to each other," I grimaced back.

The mother cat gathered her four children and explained what happened to their brother.

"Someone bought him and now he has gone to live with them. One day soon you will all go to live with new families and you all will experience so much that you will soon forget about each other, this apartment, and even me."

This made the kittens very sad and they all started to cry, especially the little kitten. "I'm not leaving," she meowed that evening as she nestled closer to her mother and dozed off.

Their mother just sighed as she wrapped her thick bushy black *tail around her children and fell asleep.*

"Aunt Laura," Stevie said quietly (only a three-year-old can pronounce my name correctly!) "I'm scared of skunks."

"Huh?"

"The mom is a skunk," he whispered.

"No, Stevie, she just has a black tail. She's not a skunk," I assured him.

"Skunks want to eat me," he said.

"No they don't," I smirked.

"Yes. There was one in my bedroom last night," he whispered again.

"That must have been your cat Rocky," I reassured him.

"No, it was a skunk and it tried to eat me."
"Stevie, skunks don't eat people. They spray people with stinky stuff that's hard to remove, but they don't eat people."

"Then I am not afraid of the one in my room at night?" he asked me.

"I guess not, since it's a cat!"

"Well, can we go visit them then?" his eyes lit with excitement.

"Who?"

"The skunks!" he exclaimed.

"No! Can I continue the story?"

"Okay."

That was the last night all the kittens spent together. When the little kitten finally awoke the next day, she was saddened to find her older brother had been sold that morning.

"It's not right," she told her sisters over their lunch bowl of kibble and tuna bits. "Why do strangers get to pick us? We should be able to pick them. That way we get one we like," she mumbled over a mouthful.

"Don't talk with food in your mouth, little kitten. No one will ever want you if you don't display some manners," her mother said while bathing kitten's older sister.

"Maybe I don't want any person to want me," she muttered

back at her mother.

"Kitten, I know how hard this is to understand, but trust me, it will be better for you if you live with a new family," her mother spoke softly in her ear as she left the room.

"I know how we can stay together," kitten whispered as soon as mother was out of ear shot. "It's really simple—we'll just misbehave whenever anyone comes to buy one of us. Then we'll always be together!" she exclaimed through another bite of kibble.

"We can't, little kitten," her older sister said stretching out in the sun's rays peeking through the curtains.

This tugged at the little bird's heart. "It's hard to say, little one. You're a kitten, and people love kittens. Chances are good that you'll be adopted, but you might be given as a present to some little kid. Little kids can be a ruff group of creatures."

"I thought kids were little goats—I didn't know they could adopt kittens," the little kitten had a puzzled look on its face.

"No, no!" the bird chuckled. "Not goats. Kids as in humans. Umm, how do you kittens refer to them – oh yes! Little strangers."

"Oh," the little kitten said. "So being adopted is good, unless it's by a real little stranger. Is that the scary part?"

"Oh no, little kitten, that's the good part. The scary part is a lot worse than a little stranger tugging on your tail."

The bird took a moment before he spoke again; he had to make up his mind whether or not to tell the little kitten the real scary part. "Well, little one, see, if you're not adopted after a few weeks, they have to make room for other animals and well... they uh...well, they put you to...to sleep," he cringed at the thought.

But the little kitten didn't understand what 'to sleep' really meant and she laughed at the old bird's sentimentality, "Bird, what's so bad about that—we sleep every night. Matter-of-fact, I woke you from sleep."

"You don't understand, little one. To be put to sleep means you never wake up again—ever!"

"What?" the news sunk into the kitten's little mind. "You mean they'll kill me?"

"Strangers like to say sleep—it makes them feel better about the whole thing," the bird explained.

"Well, forget that! I'm not hanging around to find out what they're going to do with me," the kitten stormed off into the next room.

"Wait, kitten," the bird yelled after her. "What are you going to do? Nothing crazy, I hope? Don't run away. Worse things could happen to you outside. There's no guarantee they'll put you to sleep."
The little kitten stopped in the doorway, "There's no guarantee they won't put me to sleep."

"But kitten, it's very cold this time of year, you could freeze and there are wild dogs out there..."

"In New Baltimore?" Mandy just looked at me.

"Okay, let me change that..."

"There are stray dogs out there – you could be injured.

There isn't always a meal waiting for you—you could starve—and there are people out there that don't like cats—they could be mean to you. The pound is at least, warm and safe. Some nice stranger might adopt you."

"And then, they may not," the little kitten finished the birds sentence. "Look bird, I really appreciate your concern, but I'd

rather have the chance to find something than one chance for someone to find me."

With that said, the little kitten began to plan her escape from the little apartment, and it just-so-happened that very next morning.

She kissed her mother good-bye, bid farewell to the bird, and took her place, in the cold, dark hall at the front door. Almost every day the owner of the apartment was in such a hurry to exit the little apartment, she never paid attention to what was occurring around her, and that morning was like all the others. So, when the lady ran out the door, the little kitten ran out too.

The wind was crisp and blew harshly at the kittens' soft fur. All that green stuff that lays around on the ground was hard and sparkly and it made a crackling sound under her small paws. When all the excitement of the escape had subsided the little kitten sat back down on the steps of the apartment to think. The plan had worked perfectly but she hadn't thought any further than her decampment.

"What's that?" Michael asked.

"What?"

"Decampment."

"It's like escaping."

After a few minutes, she decided to just start walking. She knew some of her surroundings from looking out the window of the apartment, but she just didn't know what was which way. So, she followed her nose and the noise and soon found the town. Not wanting to be recaptured, she took the alley to avoid all strangers and stayed hidden in all the brush behind the buildings. After a few hour of spying on the happenings of the town, her little tummy began to growl, and when she lived at the apartment when this occurred, she would just go to the room with food, so she let her stomach talk until she couldn't stand it anymore. She could smell something tasty not far away, lingering in the air.

Her little feet carried her to the source of the delicious odor, but when she arrived there, she was met by dozens of black birds, sparrows and a few squirrels.

"What a funny looking squirrel," the black birds laughed. "I've never seen a while spotted one before," one of the birds teased.

"And with such a scrawny tail," another bird added while pecking at the little kitten's tail.

The kitten swatted at the birds gathering around her, meowing, "Leave me alone!"

But the birds persisted in their pestering, "look at it. It's a disgrace to all squirrel kind."

"It is not one of us," someone muttered.

"What?" the bird balked.

"It is not a squirrel," another voice muttered.

"Who said that?" the birds looked around.

"We did," two squirrels chattered, while converging on the crowd of birds.

"What do you mean?" one of the black birds questioned.

"It's not a squirrel," they repeated taking a closer look at the kitten.

"What?" the bird squawked.

"Do you need me to speak S-L-O-W-E-R? This is not a squirrel," the larger of the two rodents said.

"It is a .... a...," the other squirrel looked in the kittens face, "Cat!"

At that, the birds took flight and the squirrels scurried up a tree. The little kitten wasn't exactly sure why they ran, but she was glad they had gone.

She made her way over to the giant trash cans the other animals had been eating out of, and began munching on a piece of stale bread laying on the ground. It wasn't nearly as good as the food she'd have at home, but it was food – that's all her stomach cared about. While eating, a small sparrow swooped down next to her looking for some left-over morsels of food.

"Go away," the little kitten said to the sparrow.

"No," the sparrow tweeted, coming closer to her.

"There's no food for you," the kitten meowed.

"You've got some under your paws," the sparrow moved closer.

"Cat!" the kitten yelled remembering what the squirrel had said before all the animals ran away.

"Bird!" the sparrow shouted back, not knowing why the cat was shouting.

"Aren't you going to fly away?"

"No," the sparrow hopped closer.

"Why not?" the kitten was confused.

"I'm hungry!"

"But I yelled 'Cat!'"

"Yeah, and I yelled 'Bird!'"

"But earlier when that squirrel yelled 'Cat' everyone ran away—aren't you scared?"

"Oh, I thought you were introducing yourself—anyway, why would I be frightened of a little kitten?" the sparrow asked.

"Well, I just figured..."

"Yeah, whatever—you gonna eat all that?" the sparrow motioned towards the bread the kitten was hoarding.

"Maybe."

"Come on. Share with your old pal, Joe," the sparrow said throwing his wing around the little kitten.

"Who is he?" she inquired.

"Me," he said stealing a bite of her bread. "Oh, thughis es myb grosh," he took another bite.

"Well, I suppose you can have some of my bread, since you've just about eaten it all," the little kitten handed over the bread.

"Kitten, kitten, kitten. This here bread is public domain – that means that everybody and anybody –who wants to fight for it. Just be glad it was me, your old friend Joe, here with you, breaking this bread and not some mean dog, rippin it out of your mouth. Right now is when I'd break into song, if we were in a movie, but we're not, so I won't!" The bird kept eating, "I can't beweave yo gabe me dis. Yumm! Youb mo wha? Youb obay!"

So Joe, the sparrow, and the little kitten became friends, but when night began its decent upon the city, Joe flew back to his warm nest in the trees and left the little kitten all alone.

"You'll be all right, kid. Look at all that fur you got. Just lay down in them leaves over there, and I'll see ya in the morning," Joe said before he left her.

The little kitten laid herself down, happy with the results of her first day of freedom. At first the leaves were nice and comfortable, but as the night progressed, the temperature dropped quite low. The little kitten did more shivering than sleeping, and was up wandering around, trying to find warmth.

Maybe the bird back home was right she thought sitting on the bench watching the sun come up—maybe she'd have better chances at the pound. Her little body ached from the cold as her tummy began its nagging and groaning. She went back to the spot she found food at yesterday but there wasn't any.

"It only comes here once a week, kid, and then it's gone," an older squirrel shouted from a tree.

"Why is that?" she wondered out loud.

"That's just the way things work around here," he answered, then made his way back up the tree to his nest.

By noon that day, the kitten still had not eaten, and her tummy talked so much, it made her sick. She stopped under a car to rest for a moment, but when the car started, it startled her. She ran and ran and ran—as fast and as far as could, and *when she couldn't run anymore, she hid under the back porch stops of a house and cried.*

"Hey, kitten? Why are you hiding under this porch?" It was Joe. "I've been looking everywhere for you."

The little kitten was so glad to see him she ran out and tried to jump in his arms, but sparrows don't have arms and are much smaller than kittens—even little ones.

"C-an't b-rea-th," Joe wheezed. "Ss-quissh-ing me!" She collected herself from on top of the poor bird, and licked him clean. "I'm sorry!"

"Okay, okay! Stop with the sandpaper tongue—ouch!" he held up his wings to stop the barrage of cat spit.

"I'm just so happy to see you," she purred.

"If I'm not mistaken, and I'm usually not, have you been crying?

"Maybe a little, but I'm not going to the apartment – they were sending me to the pound soon anyway," her stomach began to growl again.

Joe handed her a piece of a roll he had found by that house's garbage cans "I see you're not an outdoor cat, are you? You know, once you've felt the warmth of a home it is hard to adjust to this outside life."

"I'm fine out here," the kitten boasted once she was full.

"You know, I won't always be able to provide food for you— you eat like a cow," Joe sat down next to her.

"But I don't want to be owned by a stranger just to stay warm and full."

"Kitten, some strangers make really wonderful owners, and once you get food, you can slip some to me every once-in-a-while," Joe laughed.

"I miss my mommy," sighed the kitten.

"I know you do pal."

The two of them sat under the porch for quite some time, in silence.

"Are you all listening?" I asked the parasites lounging all around me.

"Aunt Wanna, this story is too sad. Can we stop for a moment so we can all go hug our moms?" Krista sighed.

"Yeah, Aunt Warwee, and it's also making me hungry. Can I go get a snack?" Cassy rubbed her belly.

"I guess so. Just hurry back. I would like to finish this."
Soon I was covered in kids again and in all the food they had brought back with them.

"Okay, Aunt Wanna, continue," Markie commanded.

Joe came up with a plan.

"Who's Joe?" Kyle foolishly asked.

"The sparrow," the rest of the kids hollered. "Right!" he said as if he was testing them.

Anyway—

Joe came up with a plan to find the little kitten a home but one she chose for herself. He decided the main city sidewalk would be the best place to start, but first he had to get the kitten cleaned up. So he took down to the beach.

"Jump in," he commanded.

"I'm not going in there. It's too cold," the kitten whined.

"But we've got to clean you up – no stranger is going to want a dirty kitten," Joe scratched his head with one of the kitten's claws. "You need to be cleaned—where are we going to find you a bath?"

"Oh, a bath—that's easy—I can do it myself," the kitten began to lick her fur until it was nice and shiny.

"Perfect. Okay, here's the plan. You walk up and down the main street side walk and attract attention. Then pick your new owners and I'll follow you home. Ready?"

So that day, the little kitten went into town in her cleanliest fur, to search out the best owner, but her nose took over and the curious smells of the beauty salon led her to wander inside. There she saw many strangers and quite a few scary strangers. For every nice looking stranger standing, there was one frightening stranger sitting—with rolls and fire rods sticking out of their heads—some had blue matted hair mussed on their heads, others were sitting under giant bowls that blew out heat. She snuck out as quietly as she had pranced in.

Next she saw a man with lots of paper in his hands, all different shapes, colors and sizes of paper, and to top that, he had a whole bag full of it. The little kitten loved paper and thought about this guy for an owner, but there was a picture of a big scary bird on his bag, his hat and his coat. That bird *reminded her of those black birds that were picking on her yesterday, so she just brushed by him.*

"Who was he?" Cassy asked.

"The mail man."

Then she could smell the sweet bread from the bakery but their doors swung open and shut too fast for her to gain access.

Of course, there was the corner store, where the lady said,

"No pets allowed," and the bank, but there were too many cars pulling in and out. Finally, she walked to the barber shop, but when she looked through the window, her reflection shown back as a much larger than cat, so she went to find Joe.

"Who's Joe?" Kyle asked again.

"The sparrow," we all groaned.

"I give up Joe, I'm never going to find the right person—gee, I can't even find anybody," the little kitten sighed and plopped her behind down on the pavement.

"We'll keep looking, kid," Joe reassured her. "We'll come back every day until we find someone. Come on, the seagulls are

fishing today, and one of them owes me a favor.

The two of them were making their way back to the beach when an office door opened and the little kitten stopped in her tracks.

"This is it kid, this is it," Joe nudged her and flew away.

A lady stood at the open door of the office, and when she looked down, she said, "Oh, hello little kitten."
The little kitten rubbed her head on the lady's legs and said, "Purrrr!"

"My, aren't we friendly," the lady said, not bending over to pet the kitten because she was allergic to it.
Then, it was decided, by the kitten that is, that this lady would be her new owner, and the kitten took off running up the office steps to assure the deal.

"Oh dear," said the lady.

"This lady isn't a very good talker, Aunt Wanna," my nephews agreed.

"Oh dear! Whatever will I do? For I have a sneezing fit every time I touch a cat, and now a poor homeless kitten wishes to seek refuge with me. Oh dear—oh dear! What a dilemma," the

lady wondered.

"Better, boys?"

*But the lady decided to take the kitten...ah...ah...ah...chu—
sniffle—home with her until she could...ah...au...ah...chu—
sniffle—find the little kittens rightful owners.*

*When she got the kitten—sniffle, sniffle—to her house she
decided to name it Moo-kitty because it –ah...chu—because it
looked like a cow—with its black and white spots—but when
her husband same home and found the kitten hanging upside
down from the Christmas tree, he changed her name to
Monkey.*

*And they waited and waited for somebody to call about all the
posters they had hung around the city, but no one ever did—
Joe had taken them all down.*

*The smell of fresh bread wafted throughout the small home on
Christmas morning, Monkey snuggled close to her new family,
and they lived happily ever –ah...ah...ah...chu—after—
especially after the two Christmas bulbs she busted—the
nutcrackers head she knocked off and lost –once she stopped
unraveling the rolls of toilet paper—stopped biting the owners
when they sang or whistled—stopped hanging from the
Christmas tree—stopped attacking t hem from under the bed—*

stopped smacking them in the mouth when they brushed their teeth—stopped jumping on top of the door jamb—stopped stealing the lady's barrettes and rubber bands and hiding them in the litter box—stopped beating up the answering machine and answering the phone.

The End

"Aunt Wanna, usually your stories take longer than that," Krista yawned.

"Yeah, so will you go play flashlight tag with us?" Markie pleaded with me.

"It's 25 degrees outside—no, I will not play flashlight tag outside."

"But its flashlight tag, Aunt Wanna," Michael chimed in.

"And that's going to keep me warm?"

"I'm hungry," Cassy headed towards the kitchen.

"Hey, Aunt Warwee, guess what?" Mandy's eyes lit up.

"What?" I asked in anticipation.

"Oh...I guess I should have thought of something first," she realized a little late.

"Okay, everyone go and hide somewhere in the house and I'll be it, "I said putting the cookbook back on the shelf and counting. When I had finished counting, I sat back down on the couch.

"Aren't you going to look for them?" my dad sat down next to me.

"Nah, they know where they are."

THE END

Alfert The Christmas Turtle

By Sue Veryser

If you are lucky enough to be welcomed into her home, you will first be greeted by two dogs. One barks incessantly and jumps up and down. She has a huge butt and the personality of a Tasmanian devil (the cartoon, not the real deal). She's three and her name is Abigail. The other is a Golden Beagle that can do no wrong, the favorite if you will. She's eleven, seriously overweight; snores louder than any man can, and only answers to the sound one makes when mimicking kissing. Mandy is her name.

If you are brave enough to venture past the kitchen, you will be welcomed by 32 Ring Neck doves, (which her father refers to as pigeons), some free range, others not -- and if you can actually get into the living room, past the flurry of feathers and barks and fur, you will find, in a corner behind a chair, a crooked necked, diaper wearing duck wooing a towel.

I am writing all of this in the third person, because it makes the whole story less personal. I can be me, but not really me. So all that is written here can be simply make-believe.

Then, if you venture past the living room, and into her office, you will find a parakeet in a cage on a table, and on the opposite side of the room, there is a caged squirrel, named Pickle who is also enjoying the company of his favorite towel.

"All you need now is a Reindeer, Annie," Brett said from the kitchen where he stood with his hands in soapy water, doing dishes, and where one pair of pink Ring Necks had decided to perch upon his right shoulder.

"If the fates allowed, I'd have a pair of them," she joked from the office where she watched the parakeet play kissy face with his mirror. A lavender dove pulled gently at her shoelace -- it was good nesting material by dove standards. She wiggled her foot back and forth to make the laces dance, and watched as the bird hopped in unison with the movement, trying to snatch up those perfect nest building strings.

The house was alive with the sounds of cooing, snoring, twittering, and the occasional grumbling quack that made Yazzie famous. Actually, Yazzie was famous for loving towels, but how does one fit that into a Christmas Story?

Off in the distance, the rumble of a car with a bad muffler, made its way down the quiet dirt road that ran past her house. It was a sound she had grown to recognize as the mail lady's vehicle. In the four years she had lived in her old farm house, there in the country, that mail lady had never got around to fixing that muffler. So, as the years tripped by, the vehicle got louder and was simply unmistakable. The sound grew with its approach, and since getting the mail was one of her favorite pastimes, she jumped up, scaring the dove that was tugging at her laces, and yelled, "Mail Lady!"

Annie bolted towards the back door, sending a swirl of four doves from the floor to the ceiling fan, and causing Yazzie to disengage in his passionate plea with his towel and go running for his room losing his diaper in the process. Then she tripped over the giant pile of Beagle that lay snoring in the doorway, and almost did a header into the door jamb between the kitchen and the living room. She quickly righted herself and sprang to the back door. "Mail Lady!" she yelled again. "I hope she brought invoice payments today, instead of all those crazy bills we always get!" Brett watched the whole scene from his stand by the kitchen sink, and shook his head as she flew past him in route to the door. "Christmas isn't that many days away, and we still have a gazillion people to buy for," she called over her shoulder. Of course, she was already half way down the long driveway, without her coat, so that statement was only heard by the crisp December air.

And it was cold. From December 22 to December 23 -- the temperature had dropped 20 degrees. It was downright frigid, and anyone that knew Annie was privy to the knowledge that she HATED being cold. So, she sprinted to the mailbox, flung the door open and pulled out the stack of letters, magazines and junk mail that was wrapped around a small box tied with a green ribbon. Ice was forming in the marrow of her bones, so instead of studying her mail on the way back to the house, which was customary, Annie tucked it all under her arm and ran to the door. Once inside she did the "I'm freezing to death two step", stomping her feet and yelling, "I Hate Being Cold!!! Brrrrr......", while trying to stop her teeth from chattering -- mostly because they were not hers. Well, they were hers, just not her real ones... rather the real teeth were covered by porcelain crowns and would surely break, because THAT was her luck.

She shifted her weight, hugged herself, and as her temperature rose, Annie remembered the neatly wrapped, brown paper package she had retrieved from the mail. "Check this out, Brett," she motioned with her head for him to come to the table. As she set the letters and magazines down with one hand, she held the box out to him with the other for inspection. "Did you order anything from Shell Domes Slow Movers Company? I've never heard of them," she rattled the box. Something hard knocked against the sides.

"No, I didn't order anything from them. I've never heard of them, either." Brett looked down at the box, then back up at Annie who was giving him her patent look of disbelief. "Seriously," he laughed, "I didn't." He took the box from her and gently turned it from side to side, listening to the skittering sound it made. "It's addressed to you though, so go ahead and open it."

"I guess...." she shrugged her shoulders, and just as her fingers touched the end of the green ribbon, the box jumped out of her hands and landed bottom side up, on the floor. "What the ...? You open it," Annie said moving the box with the toe of her shoe towards Brett.

Brett just stood there staring down at the now unmoving package, then slowly bent down and picked it up. He gently untied the ribbon and peeled off the paper. Then he carefully lifted the lid off of the box to reveal a tiny turtle. Brett started to laugh. "It looks vicious," he said handing the box over to Annie who was standing stick straight with her hands over her eyes, pecking through the cracks of her fingers.

"What is it?" she asked.

"A turtle."

"No way, " she smiled. Brett was always teasing her, so when something crazy like that came out of his mouth, she had to question whether or not he was being truthful.

"Way. Hence the name of the company, Shell Domes Slow

Movers Company." He held the box out to her and she lowered her hands from her face and peered inside as she took it from him.

"He's adorable. And look! Underneath him there's a note or something." She passed the box back to Brett,

"Here, you hold him and I'll read the note."

"Why do I have to hold him," Brett scowled.

"Because you're a man, and it's like part of your job," she cooed and batted her eye-lashes.

"Fine," Brett sighed and tucked two fingers underneath the tiny turtle lifting him up and into his other hand. He smiled down at the tiny creature and much to both of their surprise, the turtle smiled back.

"OK.... did this thing just smile," Brett quizzed Annie.

"It looked like it smiled. You did see that, right? I mean, I am NOT seeing things, am I?"

"No, ummm... geeze... I saw it too. I think. This is so weird," she muttered as she reached inside the box and pulled out the note. She unfolded it, and read it silently.

"Maybe you'd like to read it out loud," Brett's anxiety was evident in his voice as he shifted the turtle to his other hand.

"Oh, right," Annie cleared her voice. "It says here: *You are the lucky recipient of Alfert the Magic Christmas Turtle. He was sent to you by an undisclosed recipient who wishes to remain anonymous. Alfert is special. He has the ability to grant the recipient ONE special Christmas wish. It can be anything you desire, BUT there are two conditions. First, you must use the wish by Midnight on Christmas Eve,*" Annie stopped. "What's today," she asked Brett.

"The 23rd."

"Is it already? Man, time flies." She looked back to the note.

"So, what is the second condition," Brett tapped his foot impatiently, looking down at Alfert.

"Right... it says here: *Secondly, the wish you make has to be a selfless wish,*" she stopped again. "So we can wish for anything, as long as it's not for us? That's just silly."

"Is there more?" Brett asked.

"Yeah, it also says *that once we are done wishing, we are to send Alfert on to someone else, anonymously, with this same note."*

"Of course," Brett rolled his eyes.

"So, then," Annie sighed, "What we have here is a Chain Turtle? This is nuts," she laughed. She handed the note to Brett and took Alfert from him, holding him in both hands and turning him back and forth admiring his colors.

"Says here, at the bottom," Brett turned the note towards her and pointed at the very small print at the bottom of the page, *"'Remember... you MUST use the wish by Midnight Christmas Eve, or...'* that's funny, there isn't anything else written. It ends with the word 'or'."

"Well...," Annie sat down at the kitchen table and set the turtle down. "What are we to wish for then? There are so many things we need, Brett. So many things that would make life easier, like a new roof, a vehicle for me that I don't have to keep piecing back together every month. But," she rolled her eyes, "the wish has to be for someone else. Got any ideas?"

Brett sat down in the chair opposite her and watched as Alfert slowly moved around the table top. Two doves swopped in and landed next to the turtle. Mandy and Abby danced on hind legs to get a better look at their visitor. And Abby, as is Abby's way, managed to get her nose to touch Alfert's butt. Alfert responded with the tail wiggle and what Annie and Brett swear was a scowl.

"Abby, don't do that," Annie reprimanded. "Here," she pulled two biscuits from the bag of doggie treats that sat on the far corner of the table, "eat these." She gave one to each of the prancing pooches.

"What are we supposed to wish for," Brett shifted in his chair while keeping his eyes glued to the turtle. "We could make a wish to help out our parents, make them financially wealthy."

"Yeah, but THAT indirectly help us too, because our parents would be compelled to give us some of their money. At least, I think they would," Annie laughed. "No, that won't work, although I do like the idea."

"World peace is out then, too," Brett surmised.

"Yes, that's out." Annie sat watching the turtle and drumming her fingers on the table. "You know, I think we should keep him. What would the harm be? I mean, the note didn't say something horrible would happen if we DIDN'T make a wish and simply kept the turtle. I have always wanted a pet turtle."

"Annie," Brett's exasperation could be heard in his tone.

"We're NOT keeping the turtle. We are going to follow the rules. Do what it says, and be done with it. I don't know about you, but this whole thing is JUST weird enough to make me fearful of ignoring it. So, let's just put our heads together and come up with the perfect wish."

"Ooooooookaaaaaaay, fine, but I don't have even the slightest clue of what to wish for."

Silence filled the room again, as Alfert walked around in circles on the table, stopping every now again to cast a glance in Brett's direction, and then turning his head to look at Annie. He was waiting, patiently, to grant the wish the two would eventually make, and with every passing second, Alfert appeared to grow in size.

Annie noticed it first and reached out, touching Brett's hand. "Brett," she whispered, "Is the turtle getting bigger?" She looked away from the turtle long enough to see the look of surprise on Brett's face.

"Yep," Brett exclaimed a little too loudly. "He's getting bigger by the minute. Oh geeze, this isn't good."

"Let's put him back in the box and think. We'll make dinner and by then we'll have come up with something."

Brett snagged the box off the counter, grabbed Alfert, and tried to put him inside.   But there was no way he was going to fit. Alfert had already grown to twice his original size.

"Yeah, umm... Annie...?"
Annie nodded. "OK, I'll get a bigger box from the closet, and we'll put him in there for now."

And that's what they did. They put him in the bigger box and put the box in the living room. While they cooked dinner in silence, both trying to come up with the perfect wish, Alfert continued to grow. By the time they had washed, dried and put away the dinner dishes, the turtle had busted through the sides of the box and was as big as the Beagle.

"BRETT!," Annie called from the living room. "You gotta' see this! Hurry, please!"

Brett rushed around the corner from the kitchen to the living room, the dogs followed him in hot pursuit, and all three skidded to a halt. There Brett stood, mouth gaping, eyes blinking. When he finally found his voice, all that came out was, "Oh no."

The dogs barked and growled, and then ran to take cover under the table in the kitchen. Yazzie, the duck, was hiding in his room, silently laying upon his favorite towel.

"This is insane! How are we to supposed to mail him on to someone else when he's THIS big? We can't afford the freight charge! And can you EVEN imagine the looks we're going to get at the post office?" Annie wrung her hands in disbelief and worry.

"I am not exactly sure what is going on here, but if we don't make our wish soon..."

"I wish for World Peace!" Annie blurted out. Her request was met with an enormous growl.

"What was that?" Brett whispered.

"I don't know. Maybe he's hungry?"

"Maybe he is growing impatient. Maybe he's suffering from growing pains. Maybe that was the WRONG wish."

As Brett spoke, the two watched Alfert double in size.

"THIS is NOT good! Let me see if I can wrap my head around this. OK, so as it appears, by all we have witnessed... NOT making wishes makes him grow. And making the WRONG wish makes him grow even faster?" Brett said scratching his head.

"That IS how it seems," Annie murmured. "You got anything better than world peace? And remember, we can't be Selfwish," Annie groaned at her own play on words, and Alfert turned his head and gave a small laugh.

Brett, arms hanging loosely at his sides, eyes bulging with amazement, stared at Alfert, then glanced over at Annie, "He just laughed at us, Annie," Brett's voice was low and void of emotion. "The turtle is laughing at us," he repeated, then looked back at Alfert.

"I got that," Annie said flatly.

The two stood side by side, holding hands in a united front, both wondering how much time they had before Alfert took over their house. Brett was the first to break the trance, "I think I have one. How about we asked Alfert to grant the person WE send him off to, two wishes?"

"In other words," Annie's mood lightened a bit, "our wish is to give the next person, two wishes?" She pondered this for a moment before the frown lines reappeared on her forehead. "Isn't that kind of mean, seeing as how we can't come up with ONE wish, and because of it we have a giant turtle taking over our living room? It would be cool if we could pass him on to someone we didn't much like." Annie giggled, but her laughter was cut short by another of Alfert's growls.

"I don't think Alfert thought that was funny," Brett frowned at the turtle.

The hours ticked by. The doves had vacated the living room for the safer haven of their cages, and as the dogs cowered under the kitchen table and the sun dipped beyond the horizon, Brett and Annie remained standing, glued in place. Alfert was now the size of a Galapagos Tortoise. Annie had given him a head of lettuce to munch on and he had finished the whole thing in a matter of seconds -- giving only a loud burp to show his thanks.

The situation looked helpless. If they didn't come up with something soon, Alfert would have to be put outside in one of the barns. He was simply getting too big to be in the house and the poor dogs.... and...

Brett suddenly squeezed Annie's hand and whispered, "I have it!"
"Then say it, and hurry," she whispered back.

"I can't. As much as I am a part of this bazaar situation, Alfert was addressed to you, so you have to make the wish." Brett leaned down and whispered in her ear, and as he did, Annie started to smile, and then laughed out loud.

"That's Perfect!"

Annie cleared her throat, straightened her shoulders, and walked over to Alfert. She bent down, placing her hand on his back and looked into his eyes. They were a remarkable blue and shined and sparkled like two perfectly round sapphires. Alfert, she spoke softly, "I wish for all mankind to know the love of God. That's what Christmas is all about, after all. Can you do that? Can you grant something that awesome?" Alfert nodded once. Brett came to kneel beside her, and placed his hand on Alfert's back.

(Lots of bells and whistles.... blah, blah, blah.... Alfert shrinks back to his original size... yadda, yadda, yadda....)

"So, Alfert, when we mail you out to the next person, won't they just make the same wish? If my wish was the "perfect wish", then..." Annie gasped, "Wait! That's the point, isn't it?"

Alfert smiled and nodded.

"If each person has to wish that all mankind knows the love of God, then one by one, the wish comes true," Brett concluded.

Alfert nodded again.

"You're a pretty special turtle, Alfert," Annie said softly with tears in her eyes. "I wish I could keep you."

"No, you don't, " Brett answered. " You have enough pets. Besides, Alfert has a job to do."

Alfert winked, gave a soft chuckle, and crawled into the box.

When Penguins Fly Yeah Right...

By Krista Duhaime-Stieger

Reindeer are drama queens. If the hundreds of Christmas tales about them haven't clued you into this yet, then let me give you my own word on it. I mean if you get the slightest indication of a bad turn in weather, they fall to pieces- refusing to fly due to reduced visibility and all of that. Add all the songs, poems, stories, movies, and holiday paraphernalia into the mix and you've got an even worse scenario: fog-a-phobics with pre-Madonna complexes.

Not to tarnish the reputations of the beloved deer, but as "the gift recipients" y'all get a pretty slanted view on the way things work up at the ol' Pole. What gives me the authority to denounce all the Rudolph idol worship? I'm an elf- the one in charge of Santa's transportation system, in fact. What's that mean in south of the N.P. terms? Basically I'm the one who makes sure everything goes smoothly on Christmas Eve and everyone gets where they're supposed to go, when they're supposed to be there. That being said, you can understand the undue stress I'm caused every time Blitzen looks out the barn window and sees a cloud in the sky.

Which is exactly what happened about a year ago at this time...

"It's a cloud," I say flatly. "Not even the rain or snow variety, plus it's a whole week before Christmas, I doubt it's going to linger around just so that it can soak Blitzen come the 24th."

I get a reindeer snort and an eye roll, "I'm not the one concerned about it, it's Cupid.."

I return the eye-roll quoting a Mom-ism, "Is Cupid sugar? Not like she'll melt".

"It's a matter of safety precaution, Ellie," Blitzen speaks as if I'm new to my job and don't know that this is exactly the excuse the deer try and pull every year so that they can sit in the barn all night drinking egg nog and playing reindeer games. "If the reindeer can't see, then Christmas gets cancelled, you know that".

"What'd I recruit that guy for then, huh?" I make the gesture with my head, my jingle bell embellished hat clinking slightly, "What's he, just a guy thrown in just to mess with the name rhyming scheme?"

"A little red Christmas bulb on the end of a guy's nose isn't going to do much to cut through the dense fog of a Christmas storm" Blitzen huffs, I just shake my head and wave him off, turning to take my leave of the deer and their annual nonsense.

"I'll be on the lookout for the dear born with the fog lamp nose then," I say sarcastically, "let me know if you start to hear word of him via catchy Christmas tunes".

"Blitzen's serious, Ellie!" I pass Prancer on my way to the door, and she grabs me with one hoof, spinning me around so that I can see all nine concerned reindeer faces staring at me. I'm kind of taken aback with this one.

It's like they're all waiting for me to give them the word a week ahead of time that they're not going to have to do their one job a year.

"I'm also serious guys. It's a cloud." I sigh in exasperation.

"What do clouds make!?" someone shouts from further back, might be Donder.

All of the other reindeer nod their heads in agreement.

"Decreased visibility and an excuse not to work apparently," I snap. "You're going to go out Christmas Eve. Come rain, snow, sleet..."

"Maybe you should just replace us then," Dasher shouts, "good luck finding flying mailmen!" The rest of them fall into a fit of snickering and guffawing at this. I'm tempted to be totally annoyed with them, when I'm struck with an idea. It's so obvious, so very simple. Why don't I just replace them? I can't help but smile.

"Fine," I shout, my arms raised in surrender and a smirk on my face, "Dasher, you're a genius. You guys don't want to work this Christmas? You guys want your snow day? Knock yourself out." Silence meets my words, then Dancer asks hesitantly,

"You're... canceling Christmas?"

I laugh outright. "Not in the least." And with that I turn to go, shouting back, "I'm just canceling reindeer! You all get the year off, congrats."
*****
It takes a lot of explaining to get Santa on my side with everything. I have to remind him of the past years and years of lazy deer incidences, explain to him that I can't take much more of their snow complaints and big egos, and finally he comes around.

"You'll have to find me a replacement."

"Of course Mr. C, not a problem," I assure him.

"I don't want any of those new fangled air-o-planes," he

warns.

No sir".

"And I rather like to keep up with an arctic theme," Santa takes a sip of his hot cocoa, "and no polar bears. Ever since that one stole my milk and cookies..."

"No polar bears".
*****

Being an elf, I've never been outside of the N.P. I've heard stories, I've been to school, but as elves, we get taught a lot of toy building and not a lot of geography. Keeping in Santa's theme, though, and being hard pressed to get through all the red tape involved in putting together a second species of flying mammal, I came back to the North Pole that day with what I thought to be absolutely perfect reindeer substitutes. There was only one problem.

"You can't fly?!?!"

I have the penguins all hooked up to the sleigh. There's 9 of them, for consistency purposes- I even found one with a sinus infection so his beaks a little pink. They've volunteered excitedly for the job, up for seeing it through even if a tornado whips up, because what's more eagerly excitable than a group of penguins? They've even got names you could make a song from- Popper, Topper, Bopper and Waddles, Chilly, Jilly, Lilly and Toddles. The guy with the cold is Constantine, but Rudolf doesn't have a very convenient name either. They seem totally perfect, until this little detail comes up.

"Reindeer generally can't either," Popper volunteers, "we kind of thought the whole flight thing was supplied or something". The penguins all nod their little black and white heads. Constantine sneezes.

I rub my temples, thinking. "Who ever heard of birds that can't fly?"
"It's a sensitive subject", Jilly pipes. The others nod once again.

I'm grasping at straws here, but all I can see is 9 perfectly good little pairs of wings, "do you think you could maybe... try?" None of them looks at ease as each nods his or her head for the third time.

It took years to teach the deer to fly, how am I going to teach penguins in just one week? I try not to let it bother me, as I motion Toddles forward and have him jump from a big boulder, flapping his little arms and toppling to the ground.
*****

It's the night before Christmas Eve and in the North Pole sky, there's a little elf named Ellie, still trying to teach penguins to fly.

"Ah... uh... Lilly... that was close?" Lilly smiles in a sad little defeated penguin way as she goes to the end of the line and watches Chilly repeat her actions by falling from the rock to the ground. I tell them to take a break- it's becoming painful to watch.

Obviously this isn't working. Regardless of their enthusiasm, penguins simply cannot be taught to fly. I'm forced to look at my other options which are what? Beg the deer to come back in a complete humiliating action? Not a chance. I need to look at my other resources. My head flits to the flying postmen for an instant and I scold myself, but get a laugh out of the thought. I wonder how Santa would feel about a flock of pigeons pulling the sleigh. He may have to just live with it, what else is an elf to do?

It hits me then and although I'm losing confidence in my "grand" ideas I suddenly know what to do. What am I after all, but an elf? And, although I'd rather not put myself into a stereotype, do elves not excel by nature in a certain area?

In an instant I'm on my feet. I call all the penguins and together we're rushing into Santa's workshop.
*****

"Why'd you call us here?" Comet demands as he and the other

deer approach the candy apple sleigh resting on the snow. The reigns are all hooked up, but empty. "Are we gathering to mourn the loss of Christmas this year? It's a shame that the storms got in the way". He's serious as he says this. All the deer hang their heads in remorse. There are all of four clouds hanging in the sky.

"The weather is fine," Santa says, making his way to the sleigh, "Christmas is not cancelled".
The deer look confused. "I'm going to have to disagree, Santa!" Dasher says, "we deer, and Ellie too, have concluded that there's a lack of visibility this year and so we won't go out for safety reasons! Without the deer, the sleigh can't fly".

"You're right for part of that," I say, "but that last bit is seriously construed." With that I give a whistle and out they come, eight tiny penguins all lively and quick, and then one that's not so lively because he's sick. They're fully equipped with their jingle bell collars and 100%, state-of-the-art, elf-made jetpacks.

The penguins waddle over to the sleigh quickly, squealing excitedly as they help each other into their harnesses. The reindeer stare, mouths open from their spots in the snow.

"You... you... replaced us!?" The reindeer recover from their shock and begin to shout various things.

"How do you expect to have Christmas without reindeer?"

"If reindeer don't fly Christmas gets cancelled!"

"The storms! The danger!"
Santa raises one gloved hand to command silence and they do as they're told. "Ellie," he says, and I step forth to address the outraged deer. I take a deep breath.

"Christmas," I say, "is supposed to be a time of happiness, of joy, of joviality. It's a time when you get to be merry. That's the Christmas spirit. That's what it's all about. I think that you guys and I have been arguing so long about this whole bad weather thing, that we lost sight of that. You however, as reindeer, have a right to be just as happy as anyone else at Christmas time and maybe after years and years of working a hard, sleepless, labor-intensive night, you're just looking for a rest. Those guys over there," I motion towards the eight jet-packed birds, "think of them as your fill-ins. You deserve a night off and you're giving them the honor of pulling Santa's sleigh for a chance in return. My job gets done, you guys get a Christmas break, and these little guys get to do what every penguin dreams of."

I turn to the eager little beaked faces of my rein-penguins. "They get to fly!" And with that, each penguin grabs the handle of his and her jetpack and pushes the bright red button that lifts them from the snowy ground. I hear their giggles and squeals as they take flight, and surprisingly I hear the "oohs" and "ahhs" of the reindeer behind me.

I turn back to them. "so…" I shuffle a foot in the snow and look them in the eyes, "what do you think?"

The reindeer seem to think, looking skyward at the penguins, and to each other. Cupid looks to the four cloud sky and shivers. Then they all nod at each other, smiles slowly creeping onto their faces.

"I think we can definitely deal with that," Rudolph says and he grins broadly up at Constantine who sneezes. The whole company, deer and penguins let out excited woops. The penguins chatter up ahead about their expectations for the trip and the reindeer begin to excitedly make plans amongst themselves for their first ever Christmas Eve party. Indeed all seems right with this non-traditional Christmas. Some get the experience they've only dreamed of, while others get the rest they deserve. Everyone's happy, everyone's sharing in the joy, and after all, isn't that what Christmas is all about?

Blitzen makes his way to me amidst the cheers and excited banter.

"Jet packs?" he inquires and I nod. "Thought you weren't made for that toy-making bit?"

I laugh and shrug, "eh, maybe I was just looking for more of a challenge. Deer managing seems to fit the bill... or penguin managing for that matter".

"Thanks." He says, with a laugh, "You have no idea how frustrating it is to totally miss out on Christmas every year. I think you're right about the whole break thing. It's like it became a chore," he looks skyward at the flying penguins, "instead of an honor."

"Yeah well, I'm not such a good toy maker, so you know... don't know how long those jet packs will last. We might need the real deal back next year..."

We both laugh out loud. "As long as it doesn't rain," he adds quickly and I glare at him. "Cupid really hates rain, I mean those clouds look pretty foreboding right now..."

"Blitzen!"

"I'm just saying... those little guys have a rough patch ahead of them..."

"I'll see if the penguins are interested in permanent-sub positions"

Yeah good idea, just in case..."

I roll my eyes.

Don't ever be surprised if you spot a flying penguin mixed within the reindeer Christmas Eve. Maybe leave some fish with your reindeer carrots-especially on days where more than four clouds dot the night time sky.

Christmas Tree Garland

By Anne Petrous

Beth woke up and felt a little chilly, she put on her fuzzy slippers and comfy rob. She wandered to the family room where she heard the rest of her family talking about the weather.

"Look at all that snow!" Mama said, "I can't believe how much it's snowed since last night."

Dad wasn't looking very happy when he replied, "It's going to take forever to snow blow the driveway," he looked towards Beth's brothers and said, "good thing we've got two strong boys to help." The boys didn't like the sounds of that, but they knew if they wanted to go anywhere, they would have to dig out their cars.

Beth wandered over to the front room window and looked outside. "Where'd all that snow come from?" she asked. "Gramma is supposed to come over today and bake Christmas cookies with me, and show me how to make old fashion Christmas tree garland like when she was a little girl, and we were going to make gingerbread houses, and..." Mama interrupted her, "Beth, with all this snow, the road must be pretty bad; I don't think

Gramma will be coming today."

Beth began to pout and tried phoning Gramma, but Gramma didn't answer her phone (Gramma didn't have a cell phone, only a land line). Beth wondered why Gramma didn't answer her phone...

Dad and the boys dressed warm, pulled on their boots and put on their winter coats, gloves and knitted beanie snow hats that Gramma made for them last Christmas, and headed outside to tackle the deep snow.

As Mama built a fire in the fireplace, she asked Beth if she wanted to help her make some hot cocoa for Dad and the boys, and then they could bake cookies together, and build gingerbread houses and in the evening, the whole family could make old fashioned Christmas tree garland.

Beth wasn't overly thrilled with that idea. "You don't know how to do those things! You weren't around when Gramma was a little girl; I want an old fashioned Christmas like when Gramma was a little girl."

"How do you think I learned how to make Christmas cookies? My Gramma taught me. Where do you think I got my recipes from? I got them from my Gramma. Who do you think taught me how to make gingerbread houses? My Gramma taught me. Guess what else I used to do with my Gramma when I was a little girl..."

"Did you make old fashion Christmas tree garland with her?" Beth asked.

"Why, yes I did, and you know what?"

"What?"

"We ate more popcorn than we strung up!" (Slight giggle).

"You strung up popcorn, why'd you do that?"

"That's what the garland is made out of, popped popcorn and cranberries. Sometimes we even added some colorful cereal."

"How'd you get all that stuff on a string?"

"We would use quilting needles and thread. These needles made really small holes which makes them perfect for stringing up the popcorn."

"It won't be the same without Gramma (pouting), she promised she would be here and would teach me."

Just then, Dad and the boys came inside to warm up and drink the freshly made hot cocoa, complete with fresh whip cream and chocolate shavings on top. Dad said the snow wasn't as deep as he thought; it was just a lot of really big snow drifts, but the streets looked icy.

There came a loud ROAR from outside, and by the time everyone got to the window and looked out, there was a loud knock on the door. Beth ran to the door and answered it. "GRAMMA!!" Beth squealed, "You're here! I knew you wouldn't let me down. We'd better get started; we have so much to do!"

"We have plenty of time," Gramma replied, "we won't get it all done in one day, besides, without a Christmas tree, how will we know how long to make the Christmas tree garland?"

"Daddy, Daddy, you have to go buy the Christmas tree! Get a really big one!!"

"Whoa! Gramma where'd ya get the snowmobile?" Adam asked.

"Gramma drove a snowmobile?" Jonny asked
"Ma, are you nuts! You could have gotten hurt!" Mama said.

"I knew what I was doing. How else could I have gotten here? The roads are iced up and there's snow drifts everywhere." Gramma said.

"You don't exactly live close, what way did you take?" Dad

asked.

"I took a short cut across the lake, lots of ice fishermen out there today."

"The roads are too bad to go out on right now Beth; we'll have to   wait a little while." Dad said.

"We can take the snowmobile," Adam said, "drag the tree behind us."

So, off the boys went to find the perfect tree and Dad went into the attic.

Mama began to gather everything to make the Christmas tree garland and started popping the popcorn; she knew she had to make a lot of extra popcorn so it could be eaten. Dad was bringing down all the Christmas decorations, and then began rearranging the front room to make room for the Christmas tree.

Gramma and Beth were busy baking all kinds of cookies. They made thumbprint cookies with cherries, chocolate kiss peanut butter cookies, regular peanut butter cookies, chocolate chip, oatmeal nut raisin, Russian tea cakes, angel wings, Snickerdoodles and cut out cookies. They made everyone's favorites. They even baked all the pieces for the gingerbread houses! It was starting to get late, so building the houses would have to wait until tomorrow. Gramma decided she had better spend the night.

The next morning, Gramma and Beth began to build and decorate the gingerbread houses. After a few hours they were done. Mama took all the baked cookies and carefully stacked them in different pie plates and shrunk wrapped them, she added a big colorful bow; they were now ready for gift giving.

Dad untangled the lights and hung them on the tree, while the boys started to put on their favorite ornaments.

The time had come to make the old fashioned Christmas tree garland. Beth was so excited! Dad made a fire and Mama made more hot cocoa, complete with fresh whip cream and chocolate shavings on top.

Gramma showed everyone how to string the popcorn on the thread without breaking it. She said to string 10 pieces of popcorn and then string a cranberry, followed by a piece of popcorn, then a cranberry, then a popcorn, then another cranberry and then 10 more pieces of popcorn; and repeat the pattern. It didn't take the boys very long to get bored, they thought it would be more fun to start throwing popcorn at each other and try to catch them in their mouths.

"Stop it!" Beth yelled, "You're making a mess and wasting all my popcorn...we have to make a really long Christmas tree garland." She demonstrated this by stretching her arms as far as they would go. They continued to string the popcorn until it was gone. "Look how long the Christmas tree garland is!" Beth said excitedly. But the boys were more interested in what would happen if they threw the old maids (un-popped popcorn kernels) into the fire. They threw all the old maids into the fire, and within a few seconds, they began to pop and fly out of the fire and onto the floor; they thought that was really cool.

Beth helped her Daddy as they carefully hung the Christmas tree garland around the tree. "Something is missing" Beth thought to herself. "Where's the angel and the skirt?"

Many years ago, when Mama and Dad got married, Gramma had crotched them a beautiful angel to go on the top of their Christmas tree. She also made them a beautiful Christmas tree skirt out of different Christmas patterned material. Mama didn't want anything to happen to these priceless family heirlooms, so she kept them in a special place in her closet...right next to her wedding dress. Mama disappeared and came back a few minutes later with the angel, the skirt and some crotched stars and bells to hang on the tree. As Mama tied the skirt around the bottom of the tree, Dad held Beth up so she could put the angel on top. It was a long standing family tradition that the youngest person got to put the angle on top.

As Dad brought out the wrought iron initial Christmas stocking holders, Gramma surprised everyone with brand new home made quilted Christmas stockings, and each one had someone's name hand embroidered on them, even the dogs and cat got a new Christmas stocking! Everyone carefully hung their new stockings on their letter located on the fireplace mantle. Since there was so much Christmas tree garland left, Beth had Dad decorate the mantle with it, and the wreath that was hanging on the fireplace.

As the fire roared, everyone admired the beautiful Christmas tree. It was getting late, and since the next day was Christmas Eve, Gramma decided to stay the night, (It's a good thing she packed a suitcase! She probably figured she would be staying since Christmas was just a couple days away).

Beth was happy with the way Christmas was turning out so far, but she wanted to know more about Christmas when Gramma was a little girl. "Gramma, what else did you do when you were a little girl?"

"Well," Gramma replied, "since I had so many brothers and sisters, and we didn't have much money, we would make gifts for each other."

"Like what?"

"Sometimes I would make special cut out cookies and spelled out their names, and decorate them really pretty or maybe a special treat like fudge or taffy. Or I would knit them a scarf, or hat or maybe mittens. Other times I made them handkerchiefs and embroidered their initials on them. For my sisters, I sometimes made them aprons or knitted slippers, sometimes a new babushka for their heads. My older brothers made me ragdolls when I was really little."

"We should do that!" Beth said excitedly jumping up and down.

Both of her brothers rolled their eyes.

And so it was decided everyone would make each other a handmade gift this year.

The boys found some wood and made a bird house for Mama and a box to hold all the TV remotes for Dad, a jewelry box for Gramma and they each made Beth a rag doll. Beth didn't know how to knit, but she could sew. She found a box of soft fleece material and made everyone scarves and sewed big pockets on them.

Mama made Beth a sparkly necklace with matching bracelet. And for Gramma she made a necklace with a matching pair of earring. She weaved a thin leather strip and attached a polished stone to make a manly necklace for Dad and the boys.

Dad made a doll cradle for Beth so her new dolls would have a place to sleep. He made Adam a skateboard ramp and a new book case for Jon so all of his video games and comics could be neatly stacked on the shelves instead of on the floor. He was going to surprise Gramma by detailing her car, and for Mama, he was going to cook her a special dinner on New Year's Eve.

Gramma made everyone lap quilts (she already had them made and actually brought them over earlier in the week). While everyone was busy making gifts, Gramma made some of her special fudge and some cashew peanut brittle.

Mama joined Gramma in the kitchen and they began to bake pies for Christmas Dinner the next day. They also got as much food prepped as they could. Tonight's dinner would be something easy and quick, they ordered out and had some Chinese food delivered.

There was a group of people that were walking down the street singing Christmas Carols for everyone to hear; Beth watched out the window and began to sing a long, soon Mama and Gramma joined in the singing.

It was getting late; Beth had Mama make some hot cocoa while she fixed a special plate of cookies for Santa, and some carrots and apples for the reindeer. She placed them on the hearth of the fire place.

The smell of fresh baked cinnamon rolls filled the air as the children woke up on Christmas Day. Gramma explained when she was a little girl, her Mama always made cinnamon rolls Christmas morning. These weren't the "instant" kind that you can buy from the refrigerated section at the grocery store either, they were made from scratch.

After breakfast, everyone gathered around the Christmas tree. Santa had come and left a note thanking Beth for the delicious cookies and let her know the reindeer enjoyed their carrots and apples.

Everyone opened their gifts and said the homemade gifts were better than the ones Santa brought. They decided they would make homemade gifts again next year.

Mama and Gramma disappeared into the kitchen to spend the day cooking Christmas dinner; maple glazed ham, real mash potatoes with gravy, bacon wrapped asparagus, green beans with almonds, Cesar salad, fresh baked rolls and bread, fresh churned butter and a variety of pies with fresh whip cream.

"This was the best Christmas EVER!" Beth said.

A few days had passed and it was time to take down the tree. Beth called Gramma, since she finally went home, "Gramma, what should I do with the old fashioned Christmas tree garland?" and Gramma replied, "Hang it from the bushes and trees outside, it will be a special treat for the birds and any other little critter that's out there." So that's what Beth did, she carefully strung the old fashioned Christmas tree garland all around the back yard.

Beth began to think about what gifts she would make for next Christmas, as well as how long next year's Christmas tree garland should be. She also thought about the day when she would have children of her own and would be able to continue these new family traditions...

A Family Tree

By Jade Meadows

November 20

Dear Diary,

Once upon a time, there was a lush green forest in a magical land called "Oregon." This beautiful forest is home to far too many to count. I can vouch for how unbelievable it is, seeing as how it's my home too. Or at least it was. Everything changed this morning, like it does during the end of autumn every single year. Annually, a group of men come into the forest and start brutally injuring dozens of my family members and friends. After they're finished with their horrid ritual, they pile all of the victims on a huge truck and take them away. We never see them again. Everyone in the forest has lost someone to these barbarians. Can you imagine how horrible that is for us residents of the forest? Watching your friends and family tortured and taken away every year? Imagine everything is going great, you're being completely normal, and the next minute, all of the sudden, you witness your loved ones being cut down in their prime. Literally cut down. The men use a chainsaw. Oh wait. Did I not tell you that I'm a tree? Wow, looking back at this entry and reading it while thinking I'm a human... That makes it extremely dark and mildly uncomfortable. So... sorry about that.

Anyways, I'm a tree. A Douglas fir tree to be exact, just in case you were wondering. My name is Trevor. Trevor Green. Like "evergreen," but with a Trevor. Around this time, every year, this group of men (lumberjacks is what my papatree always called them) come into our forest, and start con*tree*buting to deforestation. One of the worst parts is that they have one certain type of tree that they target every year. They don't go for the really young trees, and they don't bother trying to take down the down the centuries old gargantuan trees in our forest. No, they go straight for the adolescents. The ones that can no longer be called children, but are nowhere close to being full grown. If you're over eight feet tall, but smaller than about twelve feet tall, you have a genuine *tree*ason to be afraid when the humans come.

Something that makes it even scarier is that we have no idea what they're going to do with us. Humans use us, or at least our lumber, for tons of things. Buildings, homes, furniture just to name a few. But if you're *tree*ally unlucky, you might get turned into something like paper. My old grandtree used to tell us that when they turn trees into paper, they slice your wood into a sheet so thin that you can actually see through it! Getting cut down is one thing, but having your body sliced up over and over and over again? That's a whole new level of cruel. So all we can do for those that get taken away is pray to Godtree and hope he's listening.

So, this year I'm about ten feet tall. That's about a foot taller than all the other trees my age. See, I'm in love with a pine named Annie Oaktree. She's beautiful in every single way. She has the longest branches that are just full of luscious green pine needles. She has the smoothest bark you've ever seen, the color of a doe's gleaming coat, and don't even get me *started* on her pine cones. We've been exchanging pleasan*trees* over *tree*mail, but now it's time to talk in person. She could date any tree she wants to. And this year, with my 12 inch height advantage to make me stand out, she was going to pick me. I was so excited to see Annie Oaktree that I didn't notice how tense everyone was. I should've picked up on the mood. It was like the anxiety was in the air. Everyone was quieter than usual, just waiting for those lumberjacks to come and drastically alter our world by ending the lives of hundreds of our friends and family members yet again. Also, if I had been paying attention, I probably would have noticed the gnawing feeling that I was having in the pit of my stomach. A feeling that made me sure something bad was going to happen to *me* in particular. I don't know how I knew; it was just a gut feeling. And what do you know? I was right. I was the *very first* tree that they cut down. I didn't even get to use my pick-up line on Annie Oaktree, well it's a pick-up monologue really. ("I hope I'm not BARKing up the wrong TREE, but you should go out on a LIMB and DATE me. If YEW say no, I won't LEAF you alone until you realize that I'm the one FIR you." Clever, right?) By the time I fell, I was too shocked to even panic. As they were hauling me towards the truck, my remaining family and friends wept (did you know that trees could cry?) and called out goodbyes. My old grandtree however, yelled out what I'm sure was supposed to comforting. "You're going to be a Christmas tree, Trevor!" Most trees consider being a Christmas tree an honor. I'm not among them. I actually think that trees who believe that are *bark*ing mad. I would have given anything to not have been cut down and to have a boring long life. If I could, I'd stay in my forest for the next century. But I guess being a Christmas tree would be better than a lot of the other things that they could turn me into. A *tree*llion times better than being made into paper. So as the humans loaded the last tree on the truck, I started to hope that my old grandtree was right. I was still considering these things as the truck turned on and took us away, never to see our beautiful forest again.

November 24

Dear Diary,

This morning, I officially became a Christmas tree. I have mixed emotions on the matter. I had been sitting in a tree lot for ages waiting for someone to buy me and take me to their home when a family consisting of a mother, a father, a son, and a daughter came along. If I had to be a Christmas tree, I might as well try and make some children happy. And it was obviously meant to be, because they walked right up to me and they decided that I was the perfect tree for them. So now I'm in their home. When we arrived, I find out that there is an older couple staying here as well as the family of four. Even more people definitely won't help my stress levels. Combined with my anxiety, I'd already started to feel like a prisoner here. I thought once I had been chosen, that I would stop being nervous and worried. But now, as they stand me up in a sort of bucket to keep me upright, I'm finding myself even more anxious than before. I'm about to start deep breathing exercises when I remember that I don't really breathe. But I just have to keep reminding myself that this could have been way worse.

November 30

Dear Diary,

It's been a couple days since I was brought here, and my attitude is getting worse with every passing hour. All I can do is sit here and stare at the wall. Is it called "staring" if you don't have eyes...? Not important. There is absolu*tree* no form of entertainment for me whatsoever. And on top of that, I get basically *zero* sunlight positioned in this spot. Also, barely *any* water. Just because a certain group of humans cut my trunk in half doesn't mean that I don't need water! They did put a little bit of water in that base that they're using to stand up my lifeless body, but it's not nearly enough. I'm a growing tree! At least I used to be... I need plenty of sunlight and water in order to help me grow up and be strong like my papatree was. Papatree and mamatree were both chopped down a few years back. After that my old grandtree took care of me. I always wondered whether or not they would be proud of me. Now I wonder if my papatree and mamatree were both Christmas trees as well...

December 3
Dear Diary,

      The humans and I aren't the only sentient beings in this house. There are is a creature that roams freely through the house at all times. I think it's a wolf. I recognized it because we have wolf packs in our forest. The humans (whose names I have no desire to learn) don't let Wolf anywhere near me. With how desperately they keep it away from me, I've decided that Wolf might be a vicious monster. Maybe they think that if it gets near me, it'll attack. The fact that they care about my safety made me dislike them a little less. At least they care about me, right? Maybe they aren't so bad... But I haven't seen Wolf act aggressively or violently at all. Not even once. It seems that his *bark* is probably worse that his bite. Honestly though, they might just want to keep him from peeing on me. I'm a tree, and *all* trees know what dogs like to do to them.

December 12
Dear Diary,

      A few hours ago, the whole family got together and started putting decorations on me. I feel as though I should be con*tree*buting more to the decorating. But I guess I can't do anything about it, seeing as how I don't have hands. I knew this day would come, but I wasn't prepared. In my opinion, this act is simply to embarrass the tree. In the background a movie is playing. I'm so excited to actually have something to do other than stare at the walls. But as I watched the Christmas movie, I noticed that all of the characters were anxiously awaiting the arrival of something. I would have just thought they couldn't wait until Christmas because they were so excited, but as I kept watching, everyone spoke of one person. They're anxious for "Santa" to arrive. I didn't know who that was when I started the movie, but now, halfway through, I've found out. His name is "Santa Claws." With a name like that, how could he be anything *but* evil? After I learned his identity, I knew the real reason everyone is so anxious today. It's not because they're excited. It's because they're afraid of Santa Claws! I don't understand what this horrible movie has to do with Christmas, but I had to stop watching before I started panicking about Santa Claws showing up as well. I had enough to worry about. As they decorated, they sang and laughed. It was nice to see them all so happy. When they were done, I was scared to look at myself. But I just told myself to suck it up and get it over with. I looked up at the decorative mirror in the room where I've been kept, and I have to say that I was pleasantly surprised. I don't look embarrassing at all. If there was such thing as a kingtree, I think his royal majesty would look similar to how I look now, shining from all of the ornaments that adorned him. Even though I resent most humans for all they do to my people, I have to admit that I'm happy with how *these* humans made me look. It's unbe*tree*vable. I've never felt so... Pretty.

December 24

Dear Diary,

Tonight is Christmas Eve. I can't help but be a little excited. The excitement in the air is palpable and contagious. Though there is something that has been worrying me since they decorated me with beautiful ornaments. The thing that I'm worried about is Santa Claws. The other day I heard Girl ask Mom when Santa was coming. I can only assume she's talking about Santa Claws, the man that everyone was afraid of. Mom tells Girl and Boy that Santa is coming tonight and that he's gonna bring them extra presents. There is already a ridiculous amount of presents under my branches, and for the first time since coming here, I feel useful. Like I'm guarding these presents from evil forces such as: thieves, 13 year olds, and dogs that can't control their bladders. This job is important. And not everyone could do this job. They *need* me, which I have to admit, does feel pretty nice. Anyways, when it's time for Girl and Boy to go to bed, they set out a plate of cookies and a glass of milk. I can only assume it's some sort of sacrifice? A *take-the-cookies-but-leave-my-family-alone* kind of sacrifice? Well, either way, I'm going to stay up *all* night and I'm going to see this Claws man, and when I do... Well I'm not sure what I'll do. I can't grab him with no arms, I can't yell at him because I don't speak human. Also because I don't have a mouth. If he gets close to me, I can slap him with my limbs I guess. I'll think of something. Either way, he's in for a rude awakening.

December 25

Dear Diary,

In the wee hours of the morning, I made an awful mistake. I had decided that I was going to throw my whole body at Santa. All trees have some control over their limbs. I was going to swing *all* of my branches forward with all of my power, and let the momentum take me to the floor. I will completely knock myself over and take down anyone who's around me. After that I will be at a disadvantage, because I'm going to be 100% useless. I'm not sure if it will really hurt him, but he'll be pinned for a minute. Hopefully the family will hear the commotion and be aware of Claws before he can finish whatever heinous job he came here to do. I just hoped that I could give them enough time. Godtree only knows what he has in store for them.

So at around 4:00 a.m., a dark figure approached me through the shadows. *Just a little closer* I thought. *C'mon, just a little bit further.* The second he was in range, I let out a fierce battle cry (I mean I tried to yell, but the whole no mouth thing we talked about earlier...) and with all my power, I threw myself at the intruder. Unfortunately, everything didn't go according to plan. Turns out the intruder wasn't Santa. It was Grandpa. I had put all of my strength into knocking down an 80 year old man. I think I'm gonna be charged with a felontree. I'm going to treehell. So of course after that, the plan played out the way it should have if it *had* been Santa Claws that I tackled. My falling over made a noise, Grandpa's falling over made a noise, and on top of those, Grandpa yelling as I fell into him made a noise. Well, more like a scream of bloody murder. So Mom and Dad came running. Can you imagine how horrible I felt? I had just started to care about these people. I had just started see myself as a protector and I go and do something like this. Dad took Grandpa to the hospital, but no one picked me back up off the ground like I had planned. Now all I could see was the floor. I heard noises behind me a couple times. It was awful because it could be Santa Claws right there! And not only could I not apprehend him and protect my new family, I couldn't even *look* at him. I've never been so disappointed with myself.

A few hours later, Dad and Grandpa came home. I heard them telling Mom that Grandpa was gonna be fine and relief flooded over me. I could have been responsible for Grandpa not having Christmas with his family. And he's no spring chicken. Grandpa could keel over any second and I could have ruined his last chance to spend Christmas with his family. Dad stood me back up and went to wake up the kids so they could open presents. Dad heading upstairs broke me out of my stupor and reminded that it was finally Christmas! Though I was still disappointed in myself, seeing the smiles and excitement in kid's eyes made everything better. The whole family sat together for hours, each opening one present at a time. I have never been around so much happiness and love.

After all of the presents were open, Mom and the kids headed in to the kitchen to start making the Christmas dinner that the whole family would share tonight, and Dad and Grandma and Grandpa turned on another Christmas movie (this one, thankfully, not featuring Santa Claws). As I watched the family head off to continue their day, I thought back on what my old grandtree told me the last time I saw him. *You're going to be a Christmas tree, Trevor!* Now I understand why my family and friends always said being a Christmas tree can be an honor. I don't want to get all *sappy*, but I'm honored to have made this Christmas better for this family. With the exception of Grandpa. I think his Christmas might have been better off without me falling on him... But being able to make kids and adults alike, people that I've grown very *fond* of, have the best Christmas ever is almost enough for me to forgive them for cutting me down in the first place. Though I said almost. Who could honestly forgive something like that? I'm a tree, not a saint.

The Revlon Dolls

by Wendy Doherty

For as long as I can remember, I have been the type of person
that responds and reacts to a glass half-empty. The Christmas
of 1958 was no exception. Or shall I say, the Christmas of 1958,
as I remember it.

I would have been four years old and my sister was ten. My
mother had a flair for the dramatic, especially at Christmas
time. We would wake up to the "mother lode of gifts." About
1/3 of them were unwrapped, as if to say: "These are from
Santa." From my perspective, could there be any doubt? His
gifts were always artistic, rich in color and texture. There was
almost a theatrical-esqe look to the display. It was one that
took your breath away and created its own magical moment.

The rest of the gifts were wrapped. They were average looking
and nothing out-of-the ordinary. I always thought Santa should
teach my mom how to wrap gifts.

This particular Christmas, my older sister, Sherry, and I
received 18 inch Revlon dolls. Our gifts were never identical.
They would be similar but never an identical match.

I fell in love with the first Revlon Doll I saw. She had on a
beautiful white wedding dress and veil. She had shiny dark

brown hair like my father and our neighbor, Pat. (Pat was younger and more attractive than my mother and I thought she was the most beautiful woman in the world.)

It never occurred to me this might be Sherry's doll. As if on cue, my mother explained to me that Sherry got the doll with the dark brown hair, the blue trunk and the clothes that were inside. What? The doll I fell in love with was not mine? This felt like a cruel joke.

My doll had light brown hair, similar to that of my mother's. And she had on earrings. Earrings! I hated doll jewelry. My trunk was pink, of course. I always got the pink gifts and Sherry got the blue gifts.

We opened the trunks to discover a hand-made wardrobe. My eye instantly moved to Sherry's trunk. I watched as she looked adoringly at each and every outfit. Many of them resembled high fashion.

As I recall, Sherry's trunk contained the following:

1. Blue satin formal with three ruffles, each made out of the blue satin. The formal had a purple velvet bodice with a matching purple velvet coat. Of all of Sherry's doll's outfits, this one was the most dramatic; and my absolute favorite. This outfit was beyond beautiful. It was exquisite; and I had never

seen exquisite before.

2. The second item that stood out was a negligee with matching robe. It was made out of satin and was blue almost muted with shades of silver. There was lace on the bodice of the gown and around the bottom of the sleeves. I was sure the buttons on the robe were part diamonds.

3. There was a dark blue (almost navy) coat with an attached hood. It was made out of corduroy and had fake, white fur around the hood. The color was so rich, especially with the white contrast.

4. There was what I used to call an "everyday" dress that was made out of cotton material with rich, jewel colors and trimmed with rick-rack. My mother trimmed everything with rick-rack.

5. Casual outfit - pants and a jacket.

All I could think of was "Wow!" If Sherry's trunk had these beautiful clothes then mine must have some too.
I opened my trunk and lifted the clothes looking for the ones like Sherry's. There weren't any. "What? There must be a mistake."

My doll's pink trunk contained the following:

1. Fancy dress. I cannot recall the color or anything about this dress. I only knew there was *not* a blue formal with a matching velvet coat.

2. Red flannel pajamas. It was a Christmas print and was trimmed with white rick-rack. This felt like sucker punch #2.

3. Red corduroy coat with an attached hood. The hood was trimmed with white fake fur. The coat coordinated with the fancy dress.

4. An "everyday" dress - cotton and simple, but adorned with rick-rack.

5. Casual outfit - overalls and jacket.
I sat back in disbelief. Aside from the wedding dress, none of my doll's clothes matched my sister's.

Much to the chagrin of my mother and grandmother, I whined about this. My mother was offended and said she would make me some doll clothes like Sherry's. Deep down I had a feeling she never would.

I was hugely disappointed and did not care who knew. My method of operandi was to wear my emotions on my sleeve. Sherry, always the nurturer in the family, tried to get me to look at the glass as half-full.

She made a big deal out of my doll's earrings. When that didn't work, she listed all the traits she liked about my doll and lastly, offered to share her doll clothes with me. I knew deep in my heart that was the best deal I was going to get.

The next thing I knew, my mother was sitting across from my father and said in a whiney tone: "Walt, Wendy doesn't like her doll." It was a big deal to her. My father matter-of-factly said, "She likes Sherry's better." Wow! My father was sitting across the room and he understood.

Later that Christmas morning, my father came up to me and asked to see my doll. That seemed odd to me because he had never done that before. I showed him my Revlon Doll and then proceeded to tell him everything I liked about Sherry's doll. He said my doll was his favorite. No sale! I wouldn't buy what he was selling.

That afternoon we went to Grandpa and Grandma VanWelden's house for Christmas dinner. My mother forced me to go up to my grandmother, Doris, and tell her what I got for Christmas. I listed everything but the doll. My mother had interrogation skills that counterintelligence spies would have clamored for.

Finally, after carefully wording her question so that I had to answer it in its entirety, she said: "Tell Grandma what Santa brought you and Sherry for Christmas." I was embarrassed and hung my head: "I got a Revlon Doll." Grandma VanWelden was also a nurturer. She replied, "Why, Wendy!" and gave me a huge hug. As I walked away, I could hear my mother telling the story of how I did not like my Revlon Doll.

A Revlon Doll was not something that was on my Christmas list. I had a little "Revlon Doll" but she was on a much smaller scale. It is my belief that I was too young for such a gift at that time.

Looking back, I want to say to myself:

1. Be gentle. It is possible my mother judged me too harshly.

2. I was a mere four years old.

3. The Revlon Dolls may have been far more meaningful to my mother than they were to us.

It would be great if the story ended here, but it does not. My sister's Revlon Doll always looked perfectly coiffed, especially her hair. She styled updos but never wanted to style my doll's hair when I asked.

Sherry and I shared a bedroom. She was into horses and books. She had impressive collections of both. I thought it odd that she would even want a Revlon Doll.

Sharing a room meant that she had to put up with the plethora of dolls and doll related toys I owned. There were times when I'm sure me and my dolls were not something a young teen would want to put up with.

During the winter, I was feeling down because my sister would not let me play with her Revlon Doll or her clothes.

Rather than dress my Revlon Doll in the clothes my mother made, I put on the dumpiest clothes I could find. I soon discovered my mother's handkerchiefs made great scarves. My Revlon Doll resembled a European refugee during WWII.

One afternoon, something awful and evil came over me. I removed the scarf and cut my Revlon Doll's hair. When I realized I lacked the skill to cut her hair, I cut it again and again. My heart started beating faster, my palms were sweaty and I knew this was not good.

I cleaned up my mess. Put the scarf back on my doll and did not play with her again. I reasoned "Out of sight, out of mind."

One Saturday afternoon, my mother was not pleased with the way we had cleaned our bedroom so she was coming in and supervising. Without even realizing the consequences or that there would even be any, my sister removed my doll's scarf. Busted! The first words out of Sherry's mouth were: "Wendy, did you cut your doll's hair?!" What was I going to say, "No?"

Sherry asked me why I cut it. My response was vague: "I wanted it short." But no, the questions didn't stop there. Sherry showed my mom.

My mother asked me why I cut it. I suggested my doll was on chemo. My mother did not find that at all amusing. I was in big trouble.

Of course, when my father got home, he was told of the doll atrocity I committed. I wanted to say, "Relax. It is just a doll." But I didn't dare. You never talked back to our father. If my mother could have branded me with a scarlet letter, she would have.

My sister withdrew her offer to let me play or even touch her Revlon Doll. The deal I had settled for, was now broken. I couldn't even look at the doll clothes. I was so angry at my sister for outing me.

Even the handkerchief I had cleverly used as a scarf was even taken away.

From that day forward and throughout my childhood, every

doll I received as a gift from my mother had short hair. She never forgot nor forgave this affront. Even my first Barbie doll had short hair - a bubble-cut platinum blonde.

Sherry lives in Kansas and I in Michigan. The last time I visited her, we pulled out her Revlon Doll. Her hair was still neatly coiffed. I eyed the formal with matching coat and much to my amazement the outfit was not as I remember it. The bodice and coat were made out of black velvet, not purple.

I looked through all the doll clothes in the trunk and marveled at how well they were made. My memory took me back to that Christmas in 1958 and how oppressed I felt that my doll's clothes were not designed by Audrey Hepburn's designer.

It seemed logical to me that if Sherry's doll's clothes were made with so much love and attention-to-detail, so were mine.

I no longer have the doll or the clothes, but I now realize my mother gave of herself by sharing her talent with her daughters. I also realized that the doll clothes I received were age appropriate for my age. I had looked at that glass and assumed it was half-empty and on purpose.

My mother passed away 11 years ago. If she were alive, I would apologize for my dastardly deed. I never realized that at the age of four, I had hurt her feelings.

I was sharing this with my sister a couple of years ago and she told me a tidbit about the Revlon dolls. That year prior to Christmas, my mother asked Sherry if she wanted to see what I was getting for Christmas. Of course Sherry said yes and my mother included this caveat: "You're going to be jealous."

Sherry told me she was envious when she first saw my Revlon Doll with the pearl-drop earrings. And, she was even more so on Christmas morning, when she discovered her doll didn't have any.

A couple of years ago, I found an 18 inch Revlon Doll in mint condition. She has blonde hair and of course, the pearl-drop earrings.

Thawing A Cold Christmas Heart

By Christopher Bartlett

Ten years ago, Tom Higginston lost his wife to lymphoma, and he consumed himself with work. He was practically a hermit to those who knew him, rarely venturing out of his house for anything, and always putting off social engagements. "I have work to do," he replied. He stopped giving to charity shortly after his wife, Margaret, passed. He figured his money was going to waste, since the doctors failed to find a cure for Margaret in time. Anytime he received a request for money his stern voice made individuals feel that they were taking advantage of him.

Now 2015 was coming to a close and Tom had little to show for all the time he spent alone. He had many thoughts on paper, but he neglected to publish them. They just felt so empty and uninspired to him. Not like when he used to write with Margaret at his side. Oh how she used to inspire him. It was like having an angel's voice in his ear. He missed talking to her about his writing so much.

As Christmas approached, Tom folded more into himself than usual. After ten years, he still reminisced his wife's death. He had counseling and medications. But he was bad with appointments and kept missing visits with the counselor and psychiatrist. As well as forgetting to take his medicine. Finally, he just gave up thinking there was no hope for him. He was only 40; he could still remarry. Losing Margaret left him empty though. She was his soul mate and now there was just a huge hole in his heart where she had been torn away from him. He just couldn't find a happy thought after she left, or a reason to even try to do anything other than work though even that wasn't the same after she was gone. His parents had sent out their usual invitation to Christmas Day, but he had declined citing work. As expected they replied with the message of "but it is Christmas". He just left it unread in his inbox as he kept working in the bleakness of his office in his house. He made a couple of sandwiches and something to go with them as he continued to work while he ate. Finally, as the church bells were tolling midnight with their song he dragged himself to bed slowly. He turned off the lamp which was the only thing on his nightstand and fell fast asleep.

Tom finally awoke when the sun was setting. He noticed a memory card had mysteriously appeared on the nightstand next to his bedside. Picking it up, he examined it. He wondered where it came from, for he had no memory of putting it there.

Coming to no conclusions, Tom decided to let it go and get some breakfast as he turned on the computer in his office setting the memory card down next to the computer. Since he was starving after only having a couple of sandwiches the night before. So he got breakfast from the kitchen coming back to his office at no great hurry thinking there no need to rush.

He ate breakfast slowly his attention always coming back to the memory card. Finally, he turned the computer on and inserted the memory card. Chains grew from the floor and chained him to his desk chair forcing him to look at the computer screen. As he watched the first images flickered across the screen.

A voice from somewhere said, "This is the person you used to be."

As the voice spoke, the images of his childhood, and of him being happy passed across the screen, they slowly turned to him and Margaret dating in their teenage years. To them getting married while still in college. Her helping him with his work and discussing ideas with him late into the night over coffee. Slowly she got sick but still stayed by his side and helped him and he wept seeing this. Something he had not done even when she had passed. He saw as he sat by her side through the last of it as she had sat by her side through the good times, and wept more. But knew he would do it all over again.

That same voice said again, "This is what you have become."

The images changed to him slinking around the house. Isolating himself from everyone. Shunning the needy when he could help. Tom looked on shocked at what he had become, disgusted with himself now. He could not believe he had crawled this far into a deep dark hole. Slowly he felt himself coming back to life as he realized how badly he had acted. How his wife would have wanted him to be after she had passed on. And as he came to these realizations the chains started to loosen without him realizing it and the memory card started to slowly begin to smoke.

As he made up his mind to live once more the chains fell away and the memory card caught fire. Tom tried to put it out to save what had been his savior. But alas it was no use it was gone. Though he put its remains on the center of his desk as a stern reminder in case he ever started down the dark path he had been on again. The next thing he did was sent an email to his parents saying of course they were right it was Christmas and he hoped he could still come to dinner. Though he might be a little late since he had some affairs to attend to before dinner.

Next he got up as the chains had disappeared and went and showered and shaved to look his best. Then he went over all the charitable requests again and sent them double what they had asked for. Then came what he knew would be the hard part asking, forgiveness. But he knew he had to do it. He sat down at his computer and opened up his blog. He poured out his heart to them. Apologizing sincerely. Telling them of the pain he had been through and how he had not known how to handle it.

Asking them to forgive him. And telling them he was going to change.

Tom then linked it to all his social media accounts and then checked his email. His parents said he would be more than welcome at dinner. He knew he was going to be late but he had warned them he might be. So he took some extra time to pick out some personal gifts for each of them as he headed for their house. Showing up with a sack full of gifts. Being chided that it was all too much. But he retorted that he had a lot to make up for.

From that day on he was always seen out and about for at least a few hours a day. He made sure to keep in touch with friends and family as a point of pride. He even became more charitable than before when he could be. And everyone always asked him why, but he never would tell them the story of the memory card.

Leaves

Submitted by William Thompson
(Author Unknown)

The leaves were falling from the great oak at the meadow's edge.
They were falling from all the trees. One branch of the oak reached
high above the others and stretched far out over the meadow. Two
leaves clung to it's very tip. "It isn't the way it used to be." said one
leaf to the other.

"No," the other leaf answered. "So many of us have fallen off
tonight we're almost the only ones left on the branch."

"You never know who's going to go next," said the first leaf.

Even when it was warm and the sun shone, a storm or a
cloudburst would come sometimes, and many leaves were torn off,
though they were still very young. You never know who's going to
go next."

"The sun hardly shines now," sighed the second leaf," and when it
does, it gives no warmth. We must have warmth again."

"Can it be true," said the first leaf, "can it really be true, that others
come to take our places when we're gone and after them still
others, and more and more?"

"It really is true," whispered the second leaf. "We can't even begin
to imagine it, it's beyond our powers."

"It makes me very sad," added the first leaf. They were very silent
a while.

Then the first leaf said quietly to itself, "Why must we fall?" The
second leaf asked, "What happens to us when we have fallen?"

"We sink down ."

"What is under us?"

The first leaf answered, "I don't know. Some say one thing, some another, but nobody knows."

The second leaf asked, "Do we feel anything, do we know anything about ourselves when we're down there?"

The first leaf answered, "Who knows? Not one of all those down there has ever come back to tell us about it." They were silent again.

Then the first leaf said tenderly to the other, "Don't worry so much about it you're trembling."

"That's nothing," the second leaf answered, I tremble at the least thing now. I don't feel so sure of my hold as I used to."

"Let's not talk any more about such things," said the first leaf.

The other replied, "No, we'll let it be.

But-what else shall we talk about?"

It was silent, but went on after a little while, "Which of us will go first?"

"There's still plenty of time to worry about that," the other leaf said reassuringly.

"Let's remember how beautiful it was, how wonderful, when the sun came out and shone so warmly that we thought we'd burst with life. Do you remember? And the morning dew and the mild and splendid nights ?"

"Now the nights are dreadful," the second leaf complained, " and there is no end to them."

"We shouldn't complain, " said the first leaf gently. "We've outlived many, many others."

"Have I changed much?" asked the second leaf shyly.

"Not in the least," the first leaf said. "You think so only because I've gotten to be so yellow and ugly. But it's different in your case."

"You're fooling me," the second leaf said.

"No, really," the first leaf answered eagerly, "believe me, you're as lovely as the day you were born. Here and there may be a little yellow spot. But it's hardly noticeable and makes you only more beautiful, believe me."

"Thanks," whispered the second leaf, quite untouched. I don't believe you, not altogether, but I thank you because you're so kind. You've always been so kind to me. I'm just beginning to understand how kind you are".

"Hush," said the other leaf, and kept silent itself, for it was too troubled to talk any more. Then they were both silent. Hours passed. A moist wind blew, cold and hostile, through the treetops.

"Ah, now," said the second leaf, "I " Then it's voice broke off. It was torn from its place and spun down.

Winter had come.

SANTA CLAUS? I DO BELIEVE...I DO, I DO

by Thomas Graves

As a child, I knew there was something special about Christmas. I could feel it. That feeling has never left me.

There is a unique joy at Christmas unlike any other time of the year. Of course...this totally makes sense!

Celebrating the birth of Jesus into a world which desperately needs love and mercy is cause for the greatest joy!

Miracles happen at Christmas - I believe that. They happened at the hands of St. Nicholas hundreds of years ago.

When Nicholas' parents died, he used his inheritance to help the poor and sick. His kindness and generosity were legendary!

And so we continue to celebrate the life of "St. Nick," also known as "Santa."

But my story is not about the Santa of hundreds of years

ago! My story is about Santa today.

"Santa" is anyone who heeds the call from heaven to love and to help others.

I want to tell you about a miracle working Santa who gave our family the greatest gift of all...a saved life.

Thirty-three years ago, my beloved brother was suffering from the disease of alcoholism. My heart was broken.
 I loved my brother deeply. He was my mentor, my adviser, and my friend. He helped me navigate through many childhood traumas.

When his addiction started to take over his life, our whole family tried to help...but none of our actions changed him.

I prayed for my brother. I prayed for a Christmas miracle. A miracle which would restore my brother to our family...and free him from this disease.

Alcoholism is a "family disease." Everyone who loves an alcoholic is affected. My parents, my sister, and I suffered along with my brother.

We needed help.

Our prayers were answered through the Sacred Heart Rehabilitation Center and a "Santa," named Father Vaughan

Quinn.

Quinn was a recovering alcoholic priest who ran Sacred Heart. Years before, he received the gift of sobriety himself, and then devoted the rest of his life toward helping others.

Like many alcoholics, Quinn had success early in life. He was a good student, and a star hockey player. He became a Golden Gloves boxer by his late teens.

He said that drinking heavily as an athlete was considered normal. Quinn also said that he could drink more than anyone else...but his drinking started causing problems for him.

He tried hard to reform himself. He tried to control his drinking through his own will power. He quit drinking, completed his college studies, and was ordained a priest. But as is the case with most alcoholics, his will power was not great enough to keep him sober.

When he started drinking again, disaster followed. His life began to unravel.

However, Quinn discovered Alcoholics Anonymous at Guest House, a Detroit rehabilitation center for alcoholic priests.

He admitted he was "powerless" over alcohol and his life had become unmanageable. But he learned through the 12 Steps that God could restore him to sanity.

And when he made a decision to turn his will and his life over to God's care, he experienced a serenity he never knew before.

After becoming sober at Guest House, Father Quinn discovered a ramshackle rehabilitation center for alcoholics called the Sacred Heart Center in Detroit.
Father Quinn saw an opportunity to help other alcoholics suffering from the disease of addiction. In Alcoholics Anonymous (AA), the 12th Step means that the only way to "keep" sobriety is to give it away.

To help others. Quinn wanted to do this in Detroit - so he took over directorship of Sacred Heart and turned it into one of the largest facilities of its kind in the US.

Quinn had a unique style. He bought 5 antique fire engines and a hearse and took his recovering alcoholics for rides through the streets of Detroit.

He explained, *"What I'm really trying to do is show my people that life can be exciting sober."* He succeeded marvelously.

Sacred Heart had an excellent record for getting alcoholics sober, and helping them stay sober.

When my brother entered Sacred Heart 33 years ago, I felt hope for the first time in years.

We knew this program had worked for other people. We prayed it would work for him!

Sacred Heart taught our family ways we could increase the success of him remaining sober.

They emphasized that his life depended on his sobriety. They said, *"If all he does is stay in bed all day with his head under the covers, and he doesn't drink...that is a GOOD day."*

They said, *"One drink is too many, because one drink triggers the impulse to drink again. And a thousand drinks will never be enough.*

If he never takes the first drink, he will never be drunk again."

We did our part, but most importantly, my brother did his part. He attended AA meetings every day. He got a sponsor to mentor him.

A friend with years of AA experience who could guide him and help him in times of confusion or trouble.

My brother's transformation was gradual, but dramatic. He started gaining great wisdom from AA . He had a peace very few people possessed. In fact, one day I realized he was just downright joyful...and that made me wonder, *"Could the 12 Steps help me gain peace and joy myself?"*

I discovered that Wayne State University had an elective medical rotation at Sacred Heart. I could go to Sacred Heart myself as a student, and learn what my brother had learned. This changed my life! I learned about the danger of pride. I was taught the beauty of the "Serenity Prayer," that I need to accept things I can't change. And I learned that God is in control, and I should pray for only one thing - knowledge of His will for my life, and the power to carry that out.

During my rotation at Sacred Heart, I read an article in the Detroit News asking if people believe in Santa Claus. The article said if you do, please tell us why.

This is what I wrote to them, and what they printed:

"I know Santa exists, and what is more, I know where. He resides incognito at Downtown Detroit's Sacred Heart Rehabilitation Center as the Rev. Vaughan Quinn.

Quinn and his busy elves have distributed the most wonderful of Christmas presents for the last 16 years.

Five years ago, Quinn gave my brother a chance for freedom from alcoholism. This gift has lasted and blossomed into a very happy life for him.

Kris Kringle Quinn gave the return of a loved one. He filled our Christmas stockings with renewed familial harmony and filled our hearts with joy.

Hundreds of alcoholics and their loved ones benefit from Quinn's Christmas spirit each year.
Because of Santa Quinn, every day is Christmas."

Quinn's gift continues today. My brother has led many other people to sobriety. I met someone who told me, *"It was your brother who helped me get sober.*
He took a lot of time helping me, and gave me the courage to stick with this program."

Hearing this amazing story, I asked my brother, *"Was helping this guy get sober the greatest feeling ever?"*

He said, *"No."* He said, *"Something I never even dreamed about was far better...watching someone I led to sobriety help someone else get sober...seeing that just floored me."*

Jesus' birth at Christmas was God's offer of a "second chance."

That is what Christmas is all about.
A second chance.

Father Quinn helped countless alcoholics have a second chance.
It's hard to imagine the number of mothers, fathers, siblings, friends and neighbors who Quinn blessed by helping their loved one find sobriety. I know for our family; it was the greatest Christmas gift we ever received.

So who is Santa Claus? Santa is you. Santa is me. Santa is someone with a heart filled with love and mercy.
Santa is someone who sees need in others, and sacrifices their time and resources to help.

Santa is someone who allows God to work through them to give second chances to other people.

The people at Guest House were Santa to Father Quinn. Father Quinn was Santa to my brother.

And my brother has been Santa to countless other people. I am one of those people.
Do I believe in Santa Claus? You bet I do.

The Christmas Story that Almost Wasn't

By Sue Veryser
& Krista, Mark, Michael & Kyle Duhaime (1999)

It was not like I wasn't trying to write this year's Christmas story. I was putting every ounce of energy I had into the idea, but I just couldn't get anything to come out of my head.

Watching me, sitting at the computer in my dimly lit office, trying to compose an inspirational story for the season was like watching a "Pop-Up Video." You know, with the little bubbles of information popping up around the room, telling me what to remember, and locations of where certain objects laid, that I had thought I had lost. My concentration was blown. It was obvious that I had one of the worse cases of "writers block" ever known to the literary world.

This was the 7th Annual Christmas Book. This year's story had to be a good one. Maybe it was that pressure that kept me from putting any complete thoughts down

on paper. I rushed to my parents' house, where all the past issues of the Christmas Books were stored. Maybe I'd find some inspiration there. I peered into the two big boxes sitting in an upstairs storage room; it was the room that used to be my bedroom.

Inside these two boxes, sat seven years of my life, neatly stacked and organized by week and year. How pathetic, I thought to myself. How sad! All I have to show for seven years of a career are a divorce, bankruptcy, tax audits and a handful of dream and memories and two boxes of old newspapers.

I sat crossed legged in the middle of the room and started going through the issues, one by one. Each page of every issue held a piece of me within. I was interwoven with the ink and paper. There was no telling where I started and where this newspaper ended.

Some of the issues made me laugh, some made me cry, some made me feel invincible, others insecure. It wasn't until six hours later, when I reached in the box and pulled forth the last issue from 1993, that depression wrapped itself around my heart and smothered me.

I was only 23 years old, when I took on the responsibility of owning my own newspaper. It was a dream that I thought I'd never obtain, so when the opportunity fell into my lap, I forgot to look before I leaped. All I've ever wanted to do was write. I wanted to make people think and feel, and laugh, and cry. Writing was pretty much all I knew.

So, after a three year string of bad luck, I found myself, not only giving the paper back to the guy I bought it on land contract from, but sitting in a gig room declaring bankruptcy. A year after that, I was separated from my husband, evicted from the trailer I was living in, because it was still in my brother's name instead of my own, and buying a small house, in a small town, on land contract. That same year, I somehow managed to get the name of the old newspaper back, and without a staff, or an office, or a desk, or a phone, I started publishing again.

Two years have passed, I'm finally back on my feet again, financially and mentally, but now I find myself being audited by the IRS for that year when my life went down the crapper. Figures...

I tried to focus on those less fortunate than myself. It was what my parents taught me to do when things went wrong in my own life. There are others out there whose luck is worse than mine. Although, I know none of them personally, I'm sure they exist.

Well, that idea didn't work. I was more bummed-out now than before. The writer's block was gone, but now, everything I put on paper came out depressing and sad. So,

I went home.

Geeze...only four days to deadline...I have to come up with something quick. How about this?

There was this green guy who was really crabby and hated Christmas, so he found this talking snowman and put him in a greenhouse to melt, but suddenly this talking reindeer with a bright red nose, who none of the other reindeer liked, learned how to fly and came to save the day pulling Santa's in a sleigh...

Nope.
It had already been done.
Not quite like that, but it still wasn't original.

With my knees drawn up to my chin and me head resting on them, I cried. Sometimes it is hard not to feel sorry for myself. I'll probably never be able to write again. My life is over.

My body was disconnected from my mind, making rational thought and voluntary movements a task. The day's second pack of cigarettes laid empty on the floor beside me. The fourth out of the third pack laid smoldering in the ashtray. My mind was splitting in two.

There was very little light in my small house, due to my not owning any lamps and the fact that I really couldn't afford any, and without my glasses, I could not focus on the papers that laid at my feet. But I didn't care to read them I didn't care to think or feel. I wanted to be catatonic for a week, left alone, numbed.

The streetlight outside my window cast shadows on my bare walls. I was afraid, terrified, and alone. I felt sick.
(Hey! This is pretty good. Depressing, but good).
Standing, wobbling, I pulled myself to my feet and staggered to the bathroom. As I turned on the lamp that sat on the sink, I immediately saw my face in the mirror.
"Never be forced to look in the mirror and hate what you see reflecting back..." The words echoed loudly through my head as if someone behind me had spoken them out loud.

I buried my head in the sink and splashed water on my face, trying to wash away the person I saw in the mirror. Deep breath Sue, in...out...in...I lifted my head again, but the reflection was the same.

"To end it all would be a waste. I fear no one would remember my name. But if I should perish by my own haste, I would certainly have died in vain."

Yeah... keep telling yourself that Sue. It's all that stands between your sanity and your being taken away by the little men in white coats carrying butterfly nets.

"My life stinks!" I yelled out loud. "Christmas, this year, stinks! People stink! Being born and having to live in this stinkin' world stinks!"

I turned out the light in my bathroom, grabbed the keys to my car and bolted out the door. I was prepared to tell the whole world that they stunk, and I knew just the place to do it.

Traveling much faster than the legal speed limit, I started over the I-94 overpass.

"Oh goody, a blizzard," I said sarcastically. "It's not hard enough to drive these roads with all the idiots out there, why now throw in a little snow to make it even more interesting."

Accelerating to keep up with all the other traffic, my car lurched forward and then, suddenly, it jerked to the right. I heard metal scrapping metal and could feel the car tipping to one side. Trying desperately to regain control, turning the wheel left and right, with both feet on the brake, I closed my eyes tight as my car and I crested over the guardrail and began our decent to the expressway below.
(Yeah, I know. This sounds familiar too. Just keep reading, it gets worse. I mean, better...)

How pathetic, I thought to myself again. My life is passing before my eyes, and it isn't even interesting. Bracing myself for the inevitable impact with the asphalt, I clenched my fists tight around the wheel, braced my legs, and tightened the closure of my eyes. Pain filled my mind. My heart raced. Fear consumed every fiber of my being. Tears welled in my eyes. "I don't want to die, not this way," I screamed,

"I'm too..."

Then there was silence. A deafening silence. It was a silence that was so silent, it hurt my ears.
Then...ummm...then...

*(Shoot! Writer's Block again. Now what? I can't go to press with half a Christmas story, unless I call it **The Half of a Christmas Story**. I know, I'll call my sister's kids. They're pretty creative. I'll make them help!)*

Writer's Note: The rest of this story belongs to Krista, MJ, Mike and Kyle Duhaime, who without them, well, this story probably wouldn't be so crazy.

I didn't want to open my eyes, afraid of what I was going to see. When I finally got the courage, I opened them slowly to see that it had stopped snowing, and somehow, my car hadn't crashed on the asphalt below. I was suspended in mid-air...at least that's what I thought. Looking to the left and then to the right, I saw nothing that would cause fright. But focusing on what was in front of me, I saw not one, but 50 giant, sharp, pointy, 15 yard long teeth, that hadn't been brushed in quite some time.

I quickly rolled up the windows, and locked all the doors. Why my windows were down in a blizzard, I do not know.

Anyway...I was freaked out. First I thought I was going to die by splattering my brains all over i-94, but instead, I found myself soon to be eaten by a T-Rex in a big blue bow tie, who was busy opening and closing his mouth and sticking out his tongue catching snowflakes, and playing "Blue Suede Shoes" on a big guitar.

When he realized that me and my car were resting quietly on his tongue, he quickly spit me out, but managed to catch me in his hand.

"Excuse me lady, what are you doing on my tongue? Where'd you come from anyway? Here I was minding my own business, catching snowflakes, and WHAM! there you and your car were sitting on my tongue."

"Uh...I'm not sure what happened. One minute my care was falling off the bridge, careening toward the freeway, and the next, I was sitting in your mouth. You saved my life, but where'd you come from? T-Rex's have been extinct for millions of years. By the way, my name is Sue, what's yours?" I figured I'd be polite seeing as how I was in the hands of a hugantic, colossal, man eating lizard! Ahhhhh...

"My name," the giant lizard said, "is Elvis, can't you tell? Don't I look like the king?"

"I'm all shook up," I replied sarcastically. "Now, can you tell me how to get out of here? Or, maybe I should ask that dreaded question...am I dead?"

"Not really," Elvis replied, "you're more like suspended in time. See when you decided you had nothing left to live for, and that everything in the world stunk, time for you stopped, just like it has for me. Dinosaurs no longer exist in your world, but in heaven, all creatures great and small live in harmony. God thinks you deserve a second chance, but only if you want it. The choice is yours."

"And the purpose in all of this is...?" I asked calmly.

"I'm in training to get a pair of longer front arms. I f I can find a way to make you see the light, the powers that be will give me my longer arms and then I'll be able to get into those little boxes of cheesy crackers, which taste much better than snowflakes. So, if I help you, you'll help me and all will be right with the world."

"All right, so what do you want me to do?" I asked.

"Well, for starters, we need to get all that negativity out of your system. We need to get you in front of a large group of people, so you can tell them all about your life and how bad it stinks."

And with nothing more said, and a quick snap of his fingers, I found myself sitting on a stage in front of a large audience. Somehow, this Dino had gotten me on the Penny Hoe show. You know that lady talk show host that screws up people's lives...yeah, that one.

Here I was asked many questions about my life, and why I thought it was so horrible. No matter what sad or depressing thing I told the audience and Penny, she or someone off stage had a story that was worse.

"Hey! This is my time," I shouted to the crowd. "I was brought here to get all this off my chest, not to be outdone by a bunch of people who couldn't get an appearance on this show. Now quit t, and let me finish."

But no matter what I said, I was laughed at and humiliated. Finally, I stood up and exited stage left. I found myself back in the grey nowhere with Elvis.

"Yeah, Elvis. That was a terrific idea. Now I'm even more convinced that people stink. Face it, I'm a hopeless case. I'll never be able to find my self-worth, and you'll never get your longer front leg. We can go through eternity together as two big losers. Maybe we'll be welcome on the Island of Misfit Toys."

"Hold on little lady," Elvis started, "I'm not about to give up on you yet. So, maybe the Penny Hose show was a bad idea. Have one more place I want to show you."

"Wait… I'm starting to feel like I'm playing a part in a really rotten 'B' rated versions of *It's a Wonderful Life* with a little *Charles Dickens Christmas Carol* thrown in for fun. So, are you Clarence, the Angel or the Ghost of Christmas Past?"

"I'm Elvis the talking dinosaur who needs longer arms, and if you don't be quiet, I'm going to send you back to that bridge and this time, I won't be there to catch you."

"Gotcha…no problem," I stammered.

"So, where to??

Once again, Elvis snapped his fingers together, and suddenly, I found myself standing next to a giant sign that read"

Ruasonid Ndal!
(Dinosaur Land spelled backward).

Elvis showed me where he used to live and then took me to a huge Dino-Theater. Here, he showed me pictures of what my family and friends lives would be like if I had never been born. And although, he showed me nothing that proved their lives would be better with me in them, a tiny spark of hope began to ignite in my heart.

If a big T-Rex went through all this trouble to help me see the light, maybe my work on Earth isn't done yet. Maybe there are many wonderful things in store for me in the years to come. It would be a shame and waste to have gone through all the bad, only to cut it all short before any of the good could happen to me. I mean, who could tell whether or not there was an award winning novel just sitting in my head, waiting to be written?

"Okay Elvis, my eyes are finally open. My heart has grown three times its size today. My nose is shining bright, so I can guide that sleigh tonight! *(Shoot wrong stories...)*. I mean, my heart is filled with the Christmas Spirit and I want to live and pass on what I have learned here today. Though no one will believe me when I tell t hem about you, I will still tell them about you. I will still tell the whole world about a friend who saved my life, restored my self-esteem and filled my sold with inspiration. Thank you my friend, I will never forget you."

A tear rolled down my face, and an even bigger one rolled down Elvis's. He gave me a big hug by curling one finger around my waist.

"I'll never forget you either," Elvis said softly, and remember, every time you hear a horn blow, a T-Rex gets longer front arms."

I closed my eyes as Elvis started singing, "I'll Have a Blue Christmas Without You."

Commercial Break! Count to 30 and then resume reading.

Grand Finale

Still Counting?

Well, Hurry Up!

Ready?

The sunlight hurt my eyes. Squinting, I slowly opened them to find myself sitting in my car again. Only, this time, I wasn't falling over the guardrail, or sitting in a T-Rex's mouth, and I wasn't splattered all over I-94. I was in my driveway and it was Christmas morning.

Elvis had done it! I was alive! I quickly opened the car door and ran into the house. Grabbing all the Christmas presents I had bought for my family, I hurriedly packed them into the car and started on my way over to my parents' house.

Turning on to my parent's road, I beeped my horn, to tell them I was there. Slamming on the brakes, coming to a screeching halt, I heard Elvis's voice reminding me that every time I heard a horn blow, a T-Rex got longer front arms.

"Go Elvis!" I shouted, and continued on my way up the drive.

It was a magical and wonderful Christmas, and it changed my life forever, for three months later, I had finally completed my first book and it had skyrocketed to #1 on the best seller list. Movie companies from all over the world were calling to get the rights to make my book into a motion picture, and all thanks to Elvis.

Move over Dr. Seuss, and take your Who's down in Who-ville with ya, for the King is in the house and he just happens to be my best friend.

Since all good titles were already taken, like the "King and I," and "Elvis and Me," I simply called my book —"The Christmas Story That Almost Wasn't."

Miracle on Main Street
by Ben C. Gull

Part I

It was a cold December day in the little town of Sweetwater.
People bundled up to their eyebrows were scurrying up and
down the snow covered sidewalks, to and from the stores.
Children hung onto the coat strings of their mothers and stared
wide eyed through the dime store windows, pointing at all the
things they hoped to get for Christmas. Yep...it was that time of
year again, and there was no place on Earth that celebrated
Christmas with more style, pomp and circumstance, than
Sweetwater.

Modern technology had not yet reached the small town. People
still did things the old fashioned way. And with a population of
a mere 300, I believe the town folk liked it that way. Like any
small town, everyone knew everyone else.

I suppose you have already figured out that this is one of the
coziest and peaceful towns on the face of the planet. The hustle
and bustle and noise of the city was miles away. The town was
pretty self-sufficient, so there was little reason to ever hit the
big city.

Sweetwater was always a great place to come for a visit, though
they never saw many visitors except during the summer

months. There were beautiful hotels and the scenery was fabulous, not to mention the lake being right off the major road, which made fishing easy.

The Sweetwater Coffee Shoppe was located right next to the town square on a street called Main. It was where most people stopped on their way in and out of town. It was a small but quaint establishment, with one counter across the front and booths lining the walls by the windows. The place was always spotless and there was always service with a smile. Jim, the owner, made the best coffee for miles and the sweetest donuts this side of the world. He said that's how Sweetwater got its name, after his donuts. He always said it with a smirk, but there were times when the town folk thought he really believed it to be true. To this day, I'm not sure how the town got its name. Maybe it really was Jim's donuts.

It always seemed to snow on Thanksgiving, late in the evening and all into the next day. But despite the cold and snow, the town always woke to the most beautiful sight. For during the night, while the people were tucked safe in their beds, volunteers from the fire department were out and literally painted the town. They decorated lamp posts, store fronts and even the town hall. There was red, green, glitter and gold as far as the eye could see and right smack dab in the middle of the town square stood the most magnificent tree, all decorated up nice and special. At the base of the tree sat the grandest, life size nativity scene, in three counties.

Now it was a town tradition that all the statues were put in place right after Thanksgiving, all except the baby Jesus. He never showed up until Christmas Eve.

The coffee shoppe seemed to be less crowded than usual for a Friday morning. The snow last night must have kept some of the regulars from stopping in. Mr. Cold Fingers, the town mortician was there, and Mr. Jingles, the president of the local bank was sitting with him. Art and Zeb were there too. No one was ever too sure whether these guys had an occupation. All anyone would ever see them do was sit around and grumble about everything the mayor did and why he shouldn't have done it that way. Old One Eye, the local jeweler and his son Sammy Shoestring sat in the corner booth by the window with Red, the town barber.

Old One Eye got his name because he spent so much time staring through his eye piece that his other eye was almost permanently stuck shut. It never looked silly like you thought it might, it just looked like he was winking all the time. Sammy was seven and was forever tying his shoes. It was obvious that he really didn't know how it was done, but he kept trying.

Sammy's mom, Mable, had recently passed away. It seemed that Sammy took it a lot better than his dad did, but kids are funny that way.

It was December 24th, 1920. Christmas Eve was upon the little town and it seemed by all the shopping that was going on, that no one had their gifting done early this year. The only people that seemed to be relaxed were the people at the coffee shoppe.

Most of the kids wanted toy train sets, model airplanes, blocks, drums, fire trucks and the like, but not Sammy. This year for Christmas, Sammy wanted a little brother. He wanted a little brother more than he ever wanted anything in all his seven years of living, with the exception of his mom. He missed his mom something awful. Poor kid. He was an only child and lonely a lot of the time. Old One Eye tried to take him everywhere with him in order to avoid that problem, but when Sammy was home from school, it was not always an easy task to tote a seven-year-old back and forth to work. Sammy had a sitter that watched him during the day, but he didn't like her very much. Isabella was an older lady, who tried to be as much of a mom to Sammy as she could. I feel Sammy resented that.

The atmosphere in the coffee shoppe, as I said, was quite relaxed until...

Mr. Jingles, looking out the window, bolted to his feet like someone had poked him with a cattle prod. His mouth dropped and his eyes bulged.

"Where's baby Jesus?"

Suddenly, the shop was a bee hive of activity. Everyone asking everyone else who was in charge of putting the baby Jesus in the manger and questioning why He wasn't there.

Chief, head of the fire department, walked into the shop in the middle of all this commotion.

"Aren't you in charge of putting out the baby Jesus?" Zeb asked.

The Chief explained that he had placed the statue there at 5:50 that morning on his way to work and asked what the problem was. By this time, and it had only been about 30 seconds, the whole town seemed to have gotten wind of the disaster. Glancing out the window, Chief saw what the problem was. He took off on a full run across the town square and peered into the manger. The baby Jesus was definitely gone. All that remained was his blanket and a crumpled up piece of paper. Chief reached in and slowly pulled the paper out. The wet snow had run some of the writing, but he was still able to make out what he thought to be a ransom note. He stared blankly at the scribbled letter and placed it in his pocket.

Upon reaching the door, he met Old One Eye and Sammy coming out. Chief handed him the paper and walked slowly back into the shoppe.

By this time the whole town was at the manger, all of them shaking their heads in worry. Old One Eye and Sammy walked back to their home and while they walked, Old One Eye read the letter. He was amazed. The letter was very angry and sad. It went like this:

Dear Santa,
I don't want any of the things you usually bring me for
Christmas. Skip the toys. I don't need them. I have no one to
play with anyway. This year for Christmas, I would like to
have a baby brother and I'd really like to have my mom back.

Thank you,
Sammy

When they arrived at home, Old One Eye asked Sammy, with the unconditional love of a father, if he had, by chance, borrowed the baby Jesus.

Sammy shrugged and lowered his eyes.

Old One Eye proceeded to explain, "Sammy, if you took the baby Jesus because you were lonely, that's okay, but you must understand what he means to the rest of the people in our town. They love him too. Without the baby Jesus, there is no

Christmas. Do you understand?"

Again, Sammy shrugged.

Old One Eye continued, "If you have him, you can either keep him all to yourself and live with the thought that you kept Christmas from all of these people, or you can put him back and we won't every tell a single soul." He smiled, and Sammy shrugged and began to tie his shoes.

"I know you want a little brother, but I don't think you'll ever have one. It's hard not having someone to play with all of the time, but I love you and I'll always be here for you. Now, think about what I've said and go out and play while I fix us some dinner."

Sammy bolted to the door and ran as fast as his little legs could carry him to Art's barn which was about a block away from his house on the corner of Water and Main. It was cold in the barn where Art kept his cow and horse. Sammy cuddled up against a bale of straw and from under the pile, pulled out the baby Jesus. Tears swelled in his eyes as he thought about his mom. Why did she have to leave him? He loved her so much. How could he ever by happy without her?

Sammy proceeded to tell the baby Jesus why he had taken him. It came out that Sammy really didn't want a baby brother. He just wanted his mom back. He was lonely and wasn't really sure what this "death thing" was all about. He only knew that he loved and missed her terribly. Through Sammy's sobs, the most melodic voice was heard and a brilliant glow filled the barn. There standing in front of Sammy, was an angel. Sammy gasped.

"Don't be afraid Sammy. God hears the prayers of all children, and He has sent me here to tell you that your mom is okay. She went away, because God asked her to come and help Him."

"Are you from heaven?" Sammy asked.

"Yes," the angel replied.

"Is my mommy up there with you?"

"Yes."

"Can I have her back?"

"God needs your mommy to help Him in heaven. There are many tasks to do in heaven and only very special people like your mommy can do them."

"Couldn't He have picked a different special person?"

"I'm afraid not," the angle smiled, "but your mommy loves you very much and when she heard I was coming to see you, she gave me this."

The angel held out her hand and in her palm sat Sammy's mom's cameo necklace that she wore every day. Old One Eye had brought it home from the store one day and had given it to Sammy to give to his mom for her birthday. She adored that necklace and never, ever took it from around her neck.

Sammy reached out his hand and as the necklace fell into his palm, the angel disappeared. A warm glow still filled the barn as Sammy picked up the baby Jesus.

Running again, so as not to miss dinner, Sammy stopped long enough at the manger to place a kiss on baby Jesus' forehead, wrap him up nice and snug and place him back from where he had taken him. As Sammy began to walk away, a soft light began to radiate from the nativity scene. Turning back, he saw the angel. She put a finger to her lips and winked and then slowly faded away.

The light stayed and soon the whole square was filled with light. Sammy stared in awe as the rest of the town came running to see where the light was coming from. All the people stood silent. That Christmas Eve, there wasn't a Christmas Carol left unsung, a present left unwrapped or an empty seat in church.

And Sammy... well, Sammy was going to be just fine.

Part II

Sammy did finally learn how to tie his shoes, and he went on to
teach his own children how to tie theirs.
The small town of Sweetwater hadn't changed much in the last
22 years. The coffee shoppe was still the place where the town's
people hung out. The boyz at the city garage kept busy. Mr.
Jingles was still the president of the local bank and Mr. Cold
Fingers was still the town mortician.

The population had grown a bit, but with the war on, many of
the young boys who lived here, were drafted.
This Christmas seemed very bleak for many of the town folk,
but other than the average small changes that all small towns
go through, nothing had really changed. Nothing except for
Sammy.

Old One Eye retired as the town's jeweler and after Sammy did
his time in school, he took his father's place.
Sammy even got married to a beautiful girl named Mabel
Gilbert. He fell in love with her because of her smile and sense
of charm and of course, because of her name. How could a guy
go wrong with a girl named Mabel? Remember...Mabel was his
mother's name.

He had children of his own now, which made Old One Eye a

grandpa. Joshua was 11, Benjamin was nine and little Victoria was seven. They were the pride and joy of Sammy's life.

Victoria was small for her age, but as cute as a bug's ear none-the-less, with beautiful blue eyes as clear as a fresh water stream and shiny blonde hair. She was very bright and wise for a seven-year-old girl. She got good grades, she was tops in her class for spelling, and just an all-around good girl. Her only downfall was her two older brothers who picked unmercifully on her and for all the wrong reasons. But boys will be boys. That's what Vicky's mom always told her.

It was December, 23, 1942 and time for the ritual story telling of that Christmas so long ago when Sammy was a small child of seven and learned an important lesson about love and the meaning of Christmas. They boys hated this story and never believed a word of it. But Vicky...Vicky stared wide eyed each and every year as her father repeated the events of December 24, 1920. She believed, even though her brothers called her stupid and gullible. She just knew that boys were dumber than girls. It was a proven fact.

The coffee shoppe was crowded that Christmas Eve morning. Mr. Jingles, Mr. Cold Fingers, The Boyz, Piece of Cake (salesman), Art and Zeb (the town complainers) and Sammy all took their places at the counter, drinking coffee and eating donuts. Chief flew in for a few moments (he was late), on his way to the fire station. He had just put the baby Jesus out in the manager, as was the custom, if you remember correctly, of this small town. It was a quiet morning in the town of Sweetwater. Too quiet.

Christmas shoppers seemed impossible to find. As I said, no one was really in the mood for Christmas this year. It seemed it was almost a nuisance for these people.

Victoria was on her way to visit her dad at the coffee shoppe. She passed by the town hall and entered the square which held the beautiful tree and life size statues of the Holy Family. She smiled at each of them and said hello and continued on to the manger, a small gasp filled the air. The baby Jesus wasn't there. "Oh no!" Victoria cried, "I have to tell Daddy!"

She ran as fast as her little feet would carry her to the coffee shoppe door, swung it open and blurted out in a jumble of consonants and vowels, "ThebabyJesusismissing!"

Sammy turned quickly from his seat at the counter, he recognized the voice. The whole shoppe stopped cold.

"What did you say Victoria?" Sammy asked.

Swallowing hard and still out of breath, Victoria calmed herself enough to get out the correct words. "The baby Jesus is missing!"

Well, if that wasn't enough to get the whole coffee shoppe in an uproar, I don't rightly know what would. In the blink of an eye, all the stools where empty. Faces were pinned to the windows overlooking the square.

"Yep! She's right," Art mumbled, "The baby Jesus is missing. What are we going to do about that?"

Victoria tugged at her father's arm and pulled him out the door and across the square to the manger. She beckoned him down to her height, blue eyes blazing, and whispered in his ear.

"You didn't steal him again, did you daddy?"

Sammy forced back a smile. "No Victoria, I didn't."

"Well, who do you suppose did?"

Sammy said nothing. Both just stared into the empty manger and sighed.

Well, it just so happened that Joshua and Benjamin were up especially early that morning. Early enough to crawl out of their bedroom window, down the tree and across the square, to grab, the still warm from the Chief's truck, baby Jesus. Then they proceeded to hide him to prove to Victoria that some stories are just that, stories, and are not meant to be believed when you get older.

Here comes the good part.

Sammy and Victoria raced home to tell Mabel of the tragedy. The boys were in their room playing and could hear Victoria telling
the whole story to their mom.

"What will the town do without the baby Jesus?" Victoria asked her mother. "They'll just stay sad like they already are. There won't be a Christmas this year, will there daddy?" Her eyes swelled with tears.

Sammy and Mabel tried to comfort her and after a few moments were able to at least get her to stop crying.

The day passed quickly but the thought of the baby Jesus' disappearance never left Victoria's mind.

"Please God...help me find the baby Jesus. I know it's just a statue, but the people of this town need him. There won't be a Christmas if I can't find him."

Sammy was working late at the jewelry shop setting stones in a special ring he was making for Mabel. It was a ring that looked much like the ring his mother wore when she was alive.

After dinner, Victoria asked her mom if she could go out to play. Her question was granted, Victoria sped to the door, boots half on, coat slung over one shoulder.

A light snow had begun to fall. Once in the empty street, Victoria began her search. She looked behind building, empty boxes, in the alleys and in dumpsters. She peaked in every store window, looking through the glass as she passed each one, but to no avail.

The baby Jesus was nowhere to be found.
Now, little did Victoria know, but her two brothers were following her at a distance, laughing each time she came up empty handed.

An hour passed since she began her search, her legs tired from walking and she was close to tears, she decided to get some expert help. If anyone could find the baby Jesus, it was her daddy.

Running across the snowy ground to the jewelry shop, she was able to catch her dad locking the door.

"Daddy!" Victoria panted, "I've looked everywhere. I can't find him. Please help me. If we don't find him, none of us will ever find the Christmas Spirit in time for Christmas. Please daddy?"

Sammy knelt in front of her, staring into that small face full of worry. "Okay Sunshine! Let's go look together. Where have you been so far?"

They walked down Main Street, and as they passed each building, Victoria rambled off all the places that she had looked.

Hand in hand, they walked towards the church.

As they passed the bakery, a bright glow suddenly filled the snowy nighttime sky. It was a glow that was as bright as a thousand candles and it was coming from the direction of Art's barn.

Remember now that the boys are still following and they, too, saw the light. Keeping their distance, they watched as their dad and sister crossed the street to Art's barn.

"I thought you said you didn't take him," Victoria questioned her dad again.

"I didn't." Sammy answered.

"But isn't that where you took him when you were my age,

when you stole him?" Victoria said, looking at Sammy, but pointing at the barn.

"Yes, but I didn't take him Victoria. Really, I didn't."

The two walked slowly up to the door, almost as if they were sneaking up on something.

Victoria touched the handle and pulled the door open with the help of Sammy. And there, in the middle, of the middle of the barn, on bale of hay, was the baby Jesus.

The boys were so amazed they toppled over each other trying to get out of their dad's sight. Falling to the ground in a pile, the thud caught Sammy's attention. Turning to them with a stern look, the boys knew they better start talking. The gig was up.

But, as all the commotion was happening, Victoria had walked closer, mesmerized by the glow and warmth of the barn and proud of the fact that she had found the baby Jesus. She didn't realize that her brothers were present.

Suddenly, the glow began to intensify. And in the twinkling of an eye, Victoria was staring at the most beautiful sight she had ever seen. For standing there, in front of her, next to the baby Jesus, was an angel. A shimmering glitter and gold, a real, honest angel.

The angel smiled.

"Hello Victoria," she said, in the most melodic voice ever heard, "My name is Mabel."

Sammy, upon hearing the name jolted out of anger toward the boys, stared at the angel. It couldn't be. It just couldn't be.

"Mom?" Sammy whispered, "Mom?" He questioned again.

The angel nodded. Victoria looked over her shoulder at her dad as he began to walk closer. The boys kept their distance. "Mom, how...what...where...,"that's all Sammy could get out. But not Victoria, "You're my grandma? Daddy talks about you all the time."

The angel held out her hand towards Victoria and Victoria responded by opening hers. Staring at her grandma, she felt something hit the palm of her hand. Looking down she saw the most beautiful ring she had ever seen. Sammy glanced down, it was the ring he had just spent months duplicating for his wife.

"Mom, I've missed you so much. Did you know I married a girl named Mabel? These are my children, he said pointing to Victoria and over his shoulder at Benjamin and Joshua. Dad really misses you too. He never got remarried...," finding his voice was hard, but after Sammy started, he rambled on until Victoria tugged at his shirt.

"Daddy...grandma knows all that stuff. She's an angel. She watches and keeps an eye on us."

"Twenty-two years ago mom, an angel visited me here in this same spot, on this same day, when I was feeling blue about losing you. I had stolen the baby Jesus, because I felt alone and wanted a baby brother and I figured he'd make me feel better. I've missed you so much mom. The angle game me this necklace," Sammy reached into his shirt pocket and pulled forth the very necklace that once belonged to his mother. "Why didn't you come to visit me then?"

The angel smiled again, "Twenty-two years ago, I hadn't earned my wings. I couldn't come see you, so I sent your grandma. She gave you my necklace so that you would know how much I missed you and how much I loved you. And about the baby Jesus," she said looking at the boys, "he was just as important to this town back in 1920 as he is to Victoria and this town today. He's the reason miracles happen. That's why I've come to visit you now. To show you that when the world seems at its worst, the most amazing things can happen if you just believe. I love you too Sammy, more and more as each moment passes. I'm proud of you. Tell your dad I love him and miss him too. Oh, and boys, behave yourselves. Stories aren't always made up. Sometimes they're very real." She touched Sammy's hand and disappeared.

The glow began to fade from the barn, but not before the whole town had made its way to witness the event. All stared wide eyed, mouths gaping, uttering only whispers of awe.

Victoria placed the ring on her finger, picked up the baby Jesus and headed for the barn door. Everyone followed her down Main Street to the town square, where she gently placed the baby Jesus back in his manger. She kissed him on the forehead, thanked him and turned to her dad and hugged his leg.

Bending down, Sammy scooped her up onto his knee. And with one arm around Victoria, and the other around his sons, Sammy realized that once again, the small town of Sweetwater would be just fine. His mom was right. Miracles can and do happen. All it takes is the prayers and dreams of one small child. And aren't we all children at heart, especially at Christmas time?

The Journey Of the
Phaff Sewing Machine

by Cheryl Scheur

In 1926 my grandmother Johanna Wilhelmina Schrama-Kabel along with her one year old son Gerald sailed from the Netherlands to their new home in the USA. In Michigan she would join her young husband, my grandfather Gerald Sr. Also on this journey was a Phaff sewing machine. The machine had been a wedding present and was a cherished item that would serve the family very well for many years and provided the family with added income.

One year at Christmas time during the depression there was no money for gifts for my mother and her two sisters and my grandmother wondered what she was going to do. Finally she took some paint she found in the barn and painted the girls doll furniture, took their favorite dolls and scrubbed them up and did their hair, she then took her only winter coat and cut it up into pieces and sewed the dolls coats and hats. The family had many more Christmases, but this one is remembered as the best by my mom and aunts.

This German built machine has been donated to the Chesterfield Historical Society in Chesterfield, MI where it is on display in the one room school house that my mom and aunts went to. This school, known as the Weller school was across the street from my grandparents' tulip farm, my grandmother taught 4-H sewing on the same machine in the school house.

T'was the Morning of the Christmas

by Sue and Laura Veryser

T'was Christmas morning, around four o'clock,
our father was snoring...he sleeps like a rock.

From our beds we crawled out with care,
in hopes that our parents wouldn't hear us there.

Me in my half shirt and Laura in tow,
afraid of the dark, we knew not where to go.

So we went zipping upstairs, to wake the others,
sister one and two big brothers.

We rounded the corner, and to our surprise,
was a big pair of glasses and two glowing eyes.

Laura did scream, and I jumped with fright.
This wasn't the way to start Christmas out right!

Steve awoke quickly and Katie came yelling,
"Jerry Veryser, Mom and Dad I'm telling!"
Then to us she began a warning,

"It's four o'clock in the stinking morning!

What are you doing sneaking in the dark?
Get back to bed, I'm gonna Nark!"

Laura being five and I a mere 13,
she, of course, cried, Katie was mean.

"Jerry scared us!" I yelled through the tears,
and then Laura stuck her fingers in her ears.

"Thstop the thsqueaming, we were looking for Thanta,
with all of us yelling, he'll need thsome Mylanta!

He won't never come here, if he thinks we've been bad.
If I don't get thsome pwethsents, I'm thsure gonna be mad!"

Everyone stopped, cause we couldn't find Jerry.
So far this Christmas wasn't very merry.

Together we began the search down the stair,
Katie in her nightgown, Steve in underwear.

In the closet we peered, the stairs we looked under,
then from behind us, a voice boomed like thunder.
"Ho, Ho, Ho, you silly kids,
you should be in bed with closed eyelids."

We all turned around to see who was speaking
Jerry around the corner was peeking.

Aahhh, we all gasped as we stared at the man,
he wore a red suit and had a sack in his hand.

"Go back to sleep, or I can't be here!"
And on Laura's face appeared a tiny tear.

"Thanta, it's all my fault! I woke up Thu,
I was so excited; I didn't know what to do!

Pleathse give pwethsents to my thsister's and brother's!
It's me you thshould punish, not the others!"

"Not to worry my little one, just go back to bed.
Let the visions of sugar plums dance in your head."

So back to be we all ran like lightning!
I hope next Christmas isn't as frightening!

Christmas 2015

by Robert Slivatz

Tis' a year full of turmoil
Race, riots and fear,
But the answer is before us
As we celebrate this year.

Jesus is the reason for the season
His birth special in so many ways
That preaches love for each other
Throughout our waking days.

Born unto the Virgin Mary
In a manger full of hay
But those from far and wide
Knew someone special was born this day.

Christ changed the earth
His birth a miraculous conception
We all should rejoice
I can see no exception.

Do unto others as they would do unto you
So simple in its thought
These are gifts that are given
That with money can't be bought.

Give of yourself
To those that are near
And share of yourself
With those that are dear.

Merry Christmas to all
And may your soul feel it right
To all God's best blessings
And to all a good night!

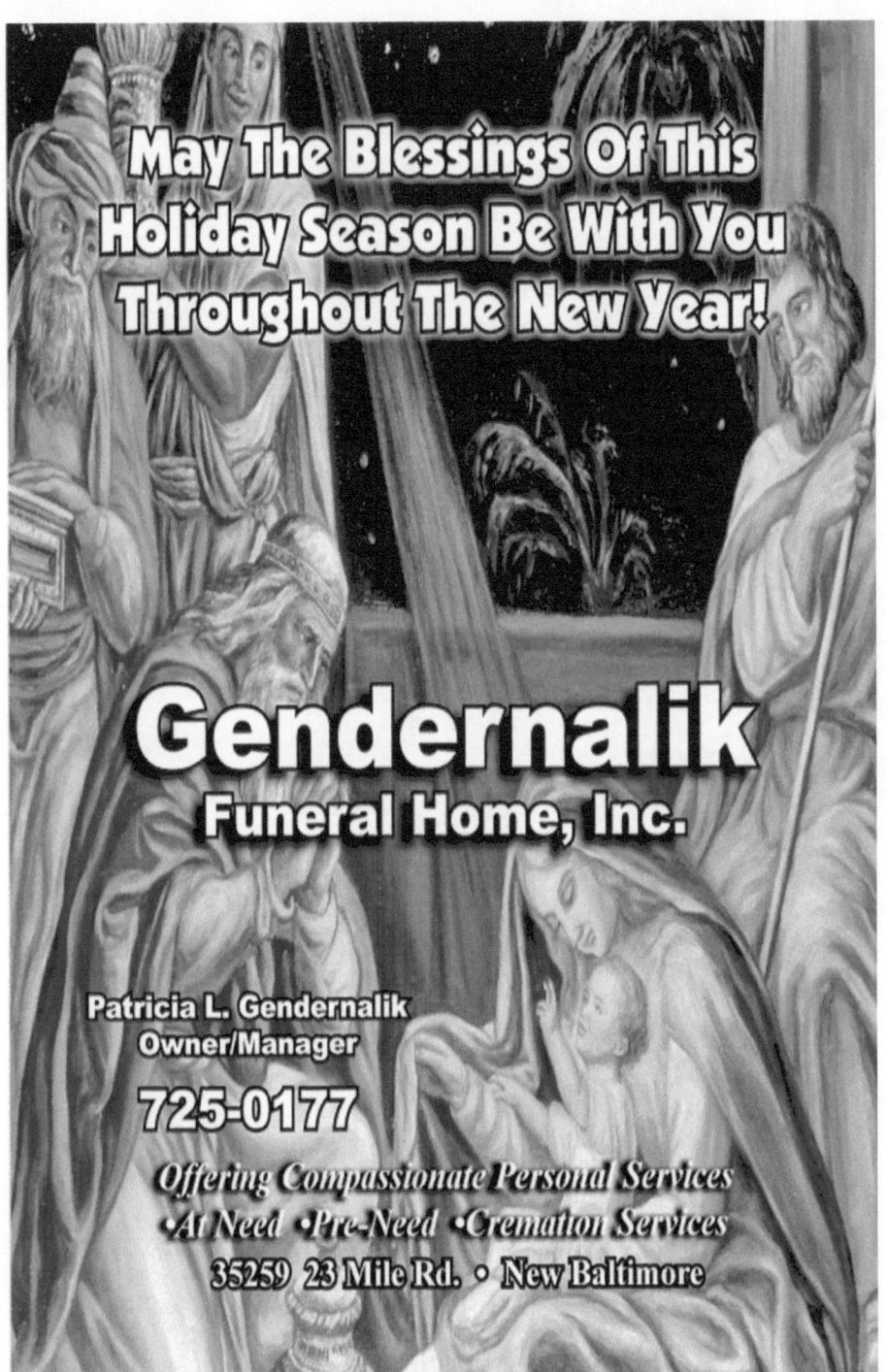

For guidelines on how to participate in 2016's Christmas Anthology, please email Sue Veryser at: slappycatcomm@hotmail.com or sue@beaconewsmag.com

This was our first one, so just imagine the awesomeness of next year's book.

www.ingramcontent.com/pod-product-compliance
Lightning Source LLC
Chambersburg PA
CBHW031216020726
47499CB00002B/610